Deference
to
Authority

EDGAR Z. FRIEDENBERG

Deference to Authority

THE CASE OF CANADA

M. E. Sharpe, INC.
White Plains, New York

The author of *Deference to Authority: The Case of Canada* is the recipient of a writing grant from the Canadian Human Rights Foundation.

© 1980 by Edgar Z. Friedenberg

The author gratefully acknowledges permission to reprint material from *The Canadian Forum* by permission of the author and the publisher; "Attica: Who's in Charge?" © 1977 by The New York Times Company and material from *The Prison: Policy and Practice* by Gordon Hawkins © 1976 by the University of Chicago. All rights reserved.

Design: Laurence Lustig

Library of Congress Catalog Card Number: 79-55935
Publisher's International Standard Book Number: 0-87332-167-7
Distributor's International Standard Book Number: 0-394-51108-5

Distributed in the United States by Random House, Inc.,
and in Canada by Random House of Canada Limited, Toronto.

Printed in the United States of America

Contents

Deference
to
Authority

1

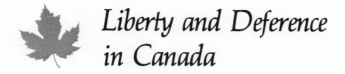

Liberty and Deference in Canada

For many years, Canada has been regarded throughout the world as one of the most respected of nations. With neither the wish nor the resources to become a dominant world power, it is not a threat to any other country. Canada is considered generous—and by usual standards *is* generous—in providing aid to less developed countries as well as personnel and material to "peacekeeping" forces abroad. When it is distrusted, the reason is usually because it is perceived as a client-state of the United States whose interests Canada is unlikely to oppose, and because its military and security forces collaborate with those of the United States. Canada's own intent is seen as benign or harmless, while its efforts to distinguish itself from the colossus to the south and evolve a policy increasingly independent of it are recognized and respected in other lands—indeed, especially in the United States itself.

Canada has thus come to serve as a nurturing force in East-West relations. It has proceeded, in the face of American foreboding and opposition, to establish firm and friendly relations with China and Cuba; the United States still has not established full diplomatic relations with Cuba. With the Soviet Union, too, Canada usually enjoys friendlier relations; it squabbles with Russia over spying and untidy disposal of nuclear garbage, as neighbors might do, but there is no real animus between them. There had best not be, for Canada is a buffer state between the USA and the USSR, though the conventions of cartography conceal this fact—the maps in our heads generally have the Artic at the top rather than in the middle where, for navigational purposes, it just might belong.

The image of Canada in the world is thus a thoroughly enviable one; and it is recognized as such. During the Indochina war, young American hitchhikers in Europe and Asia often took the precaution and the liberty of affixing the Maple Leaf flag to their knapsacks rather than the Stars and Stripes; it got them better treatment. It still does even today, almost everywhere in the world except in parts of Quebec. Not everybody abroad recognizes the Maple Leaf, but no one is offended by it. Canada is thought of, when it is thought of at all, as one of the most successful of liberal democracies, as free as any country in the world, with an enviable standard of living, a highly productive economy, and a high level of welfare and social services. Almost like Sweden, as it turns out, but with a strongly British flavor and traditions.

To an American observer, Canadian patterns of life still seem strongly seasoned by ingredients of British origin, now often gone sour or rancid—as they have in Britain itself, as the economy ages and stagnates. To a native Canadian, of course— especially if he is old enough to remember the days of Mackenzie King—the flavor of life is more likely to have been spoiled by American cultural pollution. This is not a new problem; in fact it is older than Canada itself. Egerton Ryerson, the founder of the Ontario provincial school system, struggled to keep American textbooks out of the schools years before confederation took place in 1867. Like his successors, he enjoyed only modest success.

But with reference to the issue of personal liberty, Canada is a confusing country, and especially for Americans. Many factors contribute to the difficulty, and one of these is a piece of historical deception we have practiced on ourselves, literally from the beginning. As the historian Carl S. Becker made clear many years ago in his classic study, *The Declaration of Independence*, the Founding Fathers faced a rather difficult problem, which they solved ingeniously though disingenuously in formulating that quasi-sacred document. The problem was this: in order to justify the American Revolution as a necessary step toward freedom, they were obliged to portray the American colonies as victims of a tyrannical monarchy which they proposed to supplant by local, representative government. But poor, mad old George III was not the source of the oppression to which Jefferson and his co-authors objected. Parliament was. To stress this fact, however, would have severely compromised the issue on which the American revolutionists based their claim; the latter would then have hinged merely on relatively technical points like the unresponsiveness of Westminster to colonial needs and demands—serious enough, no doubt, but not very dramatic as grounds for revolutionary action.

When Americans think about the British aspects of their heritage, they are therefore likely to think of the parliamentary tradition as the source of their liberties, which they improved upon by evolving a system of checks and balances based on separation of powers and, later, specific constitutional guarantees of human rights. This is correct as far as it goes, but the emphasis is misleading. For the parliamentary system as such provides no specific safeguards to liberty whatever apart from the promise of elections at specified intervals. This is a necessary, but not a sufficient condition of political liberty; and it is all Canadians really have. There is no separation of powers under the Canadian Constitution, which, except for the British North America Act passed by the *British* Parliament in 1867 to establish the terms of confederation, is—like the British Constitution—unwritten. The British North America Act does not establish procedures for government; it merely assumes that the Canadian Parliament will function like its forebear, the mother of parliaments—as by and large it does, though in two official, separate and unequal, languages.

Since 1960 there has been a Canadian Bill of Rights, but it is *not* a part of the Constitution. It is merely statute law and can be repealed in whole or in part at any session of Parliament; in order to get it passed at all, provincial proceedings were specifically excluded from its jurisdiction. (This was also true, however, of the United States' Bill of Rights until the passage of the Fourteenth Amendment to the Constitution, designed to guarantee former slaves the equal protection of the law, including state laws. Still, that was more than a century ago.) The most restrictive Canadian legislation, like the War Measures Act under which, in October 1970, hundreds of people in Quebec were arrested at four in the morning and detained incommunicado for weeks without charges, has been specifically excluded by Parliament from being subject to the Canadian Bill of Rights.

The doctrine under which Canada, like England, is governed, is known as parliamentary supremacy; this means that the will of Parliament is supreme in the land—the Supreme Court of Canada, for example, does not rule on the constitutionality of statutes by judging whether they conflict with more fundamental policy statements embodied in a written Constitution, as the U.S. Supreme Court continually does. Only the British North America Act possesses this authority, and it concerns itself with matters of jurisdiction, not policy; for there are held to be *no* policies that may not be altered by act of Parliament. Questions concerning freedom of expression, for example, which would be judged in the United States by reference to the First Amendment, in Canada are considered by the Supreme Court of Canada only with reference to whether they fall within federal or provincial jurisdiction—as in who has the right to censor motion pictures or license pay television. There are no areas of life that are established as permanently immune to legislative intrusion by *any* body. The Canadian court does, of course, rule as to which of several possible conflicting statutes is paramount in a particular case, and in so doing may sometimes sustain the Bill of Rights—though it seldom has.

But if Parliament is supreme in the nation, it is hardly master in its own house. The legislative function may be—and very often is—assumed by the cabinet, which the prime minister appoints. Members of cabinet are normally drawn from among sitting members of the House of Commons—and, of course, of the party in power. But they may also be drawn from the Senate,* which in Canada is appointed rather than elected. This can create an obstacle to responsible government. Under the doctrine of ministerial responsibility, cabinet officials are subject to

---

*There is no legal requirement that a cabinet member be a member of either house of Parliament, but custom strongly requires it. Anyone not in Parliament whose services in the cabinet the prime minister ardently desired would either be appointed to the Senate, as Prime Minister Clark recently did in a crash effort to make more Quebecers available for cabinet posts, or nominated to run for a Commons seat in the next reasonably safe riding to hold a by-election.

questioning in the House of Commons about actions or policies that arouse the Opposition. Question Period in the House provides the only avenue of public access to cabinet deliberations. A senator serving in the cabinet would not be present in the House or subject to such questioning.

The Canadian cabinet has strong legislative powers. Each year, about 3,000 orders-in-council, which have the force of law, are issued by the cabinet with the consent (which he is constitutionally obligated to give) of the governor-general, who represents the Queen but is actually designated by the prime minister. No further parliamentary assent to these measures is needed; and they may be either routine or as momentous as the decision to place Canadians of Japanese origin in detention camps, as was done during World War II. (In the United States, of course, a similarly disgraceful action was accomplished by military order, which the U.S. Supreme Court upheld as constitutional.)

In both the United States and Canada, people are subject to arbitrary governmental action that deprives them of liberty— though less so, surely, in North America than in most of the rest of the world. But Americans, at least, are convinced that they should not be. Despite a history of egregious abuse of liberty, of which a century of slavery and the destruction of native peoples and their cultures are prime examples, civil liberty remains a permanent and fundamental issue in American life. This is not always helpful even to the cause of freedom: it leads to legalism—a tendency to mistake due process for substantive relief from tyranny—which leaves the poor, who cannot afford much due process, without effective protection; and to excessive litigiousness on the part of those who can afford to go to court. Nor can it be said that Americans are freedom-loving people; each of us tends too often to love his own while coveting his neighbor's. Perhaps the most that can be said is that nearly all Americans have at least tried freedom, gotten high on it, and accept it as a part of their life-style. Most prefer to keep it legalized, and are willing to pay taxes on it, but not to see it become a state monopoly.

Sometimes, indeed, the grass has been greener on the northern side of the border, during the comparatively brief growing season. Americans have long regarded Canada as a potential—

and, often enough, actual—place of refuge when American policy becomes too dishonorable or too destructive to live with. I, myself, came to Canada as a landed immigrant, pompously enough, as an act of personal witness against the Indochina war and the political system that had maintained it. I entered Canada four months after a large number of my fellow Americans with poorer but more persuasive credentials had entered Cambodia, and six weeks before Prime Minister Trudeau invoked the War Measures Act, which reminded me not to be smug about my decision. My choice was influenced by Canada's generosity in admitting American draft resisters, whose position I hoped to endorse by my own action, for what little it might signify. There was precedent enough. My favorite Toronto restaurant, an unpretentiously elegant place that serves soul food, is called the Underground Railroad; it was established by blacks and is managed by them in respectful tribute to their forebears, who came to Canada as escaped slaves seeking freedom, and found some.

I left the United States because it seemed to me in 1970—and even more clearly after the American people handed Mr. Nixon his landslide victory over a decent and reasonable opponent of the Indochina war two years later—that Americans had repudiated the most superb and explicit set of guarantees of personal liberty any nation had ever established. As a social scientist, I knew, of course, that many studies of public opinion have consistently shown that most Americans would reject the Bill of Rights if they were asked to ratify it as it applies to suspected criminals or subversives (whom they view as utterly different from themselves), juveniles, or any possible source of crime-in-the-streets—that is, to almost any person who might actually need its protection. As a lifelong though diffident homophile, I had known as much without asking.

By 1970, indeed, the situation with respect to civil liberty in the United States had become a tragic paradox. Outspoken critics of the war were permitted freedom of expression unparalleled in the history of America or of any country. But this did not count for much in a nation where due process itself had been thoroughly undermined and the law-enforcement authorities were themselves committing felonies in order to suppress resistance to the war and subvert justice in the trials of those brought before the courts. The revelations of Watergate were not, after all, revelations to the war resistance movement. The Socialist Workers' Party did not need an investigation to tell it that the Federal Bureau of Investigation was systematically burglarizing its offices; and the Vietnam Veterans Against the War, in their absurd trial in Gainesville, Florida, on charges of conspiring to disrupt the Republican convention in Miami—as if it would have mattered if they had—found out for themselves that the FBI was bugging their conferences with their lawyers. Above all, there was the obscenity of the Indochina war itself: undeclared, unlawful, but presenting, in the view of the Supreme Court of the United States, which refused to rule on its legality, no substantial federal question.

During the three years preceding my move to Canada, I lived in Buffalo and taught at the State University of New York, which was one of the major centers of antiwar resistance and protest in the United States. I had ample opportunity to see the worst side of American police oppression—federal, state, and municipal—during those years. I saw friends dragged in chains from sanctuary in the Unitarian church by FBI agents, and attended the trials of others in federal court there. Michael Ferber, the youngest and most appealing (in this context, the word is unavoidably ambiguous, but he won his) of the defendants in the infamous conspiracy trial that also included Benjamin Spock and William Sloane Coffin among the accused, was a member of that Unitarian congregation. The campus itself was the scene of repeated and violent forays by Buffalo police; on Sunday, March 15, 1970, forty-five members of the SUNY faculty were arrested and charged with criminal trespass and civil and criminal contempt for violating an injunction against interfering with the normal operations of the university—minimal on Sunday afternoons—by installing themselves in an empty administrative office to await the acting president and demand that the police be removed. They were convicted and sentenced to jail by the judge who tried them, though the conviction was reversed on appeal. I ought to have been among them, but I was speaking in San Francisco at the time this wholly unpremeditated event took place.*

Meanwhile, across the river in Fort Erie, Ontario, the people, having taken no Oriental poisons, were having no convulsions and were enjoying their Chinese dinners as usual at a restaurant esteemed on both sides of the border. We used to go there often from Buffalo, too; but the probability of border hassles with drug-crazed customs officials—crazed by ambition, not ingestion—had grown too great for the meal to be enjoyable. Five years later a nightclub in Fort Erie was to become the scene of a pot bust so brutal and humiliating as to provide the first occasion I can recall for widespread public condemnation of an overt police action in Canada. Whether this can legitimately be cited as one more example of the debasement of Canadian culture by American influence, I do not know. But in 1970, Ontario seemed the very citadel of sanity. Appearances were deceptive, of course. Unbeknownst to anyone, violence was preparing to erupt in Toronto, right on the consecrated ice of the Maple Leaf Gardens itself, where miscreant hockey players would find provincial attorney general Roy McMurtry waiting to prosecute them to the fullest extent of the law. The attorney general, however—like many of his counterparts among American district attorneys—has shown no comparable prosecutorial zeal in response to repeated allegations of brutality against the Toronto metropolitan police, some of which were coldly and unequivocally substantiated by a judicial inquiry that in its report referred to certain methods used in interrogating recalcitrant subjects as "torture." Nor did McMurtry choose to prosecute Francis Fox, who resigned the post of solicitor general of Canada when it was revealed early in 1978 that he had forged the signature of the husband of a young woman he had got with child, in order to procure an abortion for her.

So, on August 25, 1970, I landed in Canada—the entry stamp on my papers says "Woodstock," which even at the time seemed too much—an innocent, six months short of fifty years of age. I could not have come to a place more likely to focus

---

*For a full account of these events, written immediately after they occurred, see Edgar Z. Friedenberg, "Report from the Niagara Frontier," *The New York Review of Books*, May 7, 1970, pp. 29-34.

new light, from a very different angle than I was used to, on the question of freedom in society and its relation to established and, especially, governmental institutions. Canadian and American practice are especially effective in illuminating each other just because there are so many similarities, for the differences are fundamental. An American who reads of a convicted criminal in Pakistan or Saudi Arabia having his hand cut off in execution of the sentence of a duly constituted court is likely to be shocked, but not very deeply; no one expects a criminal code based on the Qu'ran to forbid this as cruel and unusual punishment. To discover, as many Americans have to their sorrow, that in a Mexican court the burden of proof is on the accused, who may therefore be kept in jail without trial until the courts find it convenient to grant him a hearing at which he may try to establish his innocence, strikes a great deal closer to home; but this is the kind of legal system you have to expect in a country where it isn't safe to drink the water. Even France, which carries on endlessly about the Rights of Man, works this way.

But when a Canadian appellate court orders the conviction of a man previously acquitted of the same charges by a jury and sends him off to prison, those few Americans who notice what happens in Canada *are* shocked. I can testify that I was, from personal experience, even though Henry Morgentaler had been asking for it—by performing an abortion on television, on Mother's Day. This sort of shock, like that of an earthquake, stems not from the actual circumstances so much as from the fact that *this kind of thing is just not supposed to occur.* I have never felt this way traveling in Eastern Europe, where I knew there were no civil liberties—just wary and contemptuous of authorities who had so little confidence in themselves. And I think abortion is wrong, though not the kind of wrong that can be righted by prosecuting or threatening to prosecute the reluctant nonmother or her physician. But this action of the Supreme Court of Canada really shook me.

It shook the late John Diefenbaker, too, of course; and led to a revision of the law—but not much of a revision. The Crown can still appeal against any acquittal if it can find a point of law to hang the appeal on, and there always is one; no judge is a perfect legal technician. If it wins, the defendant will not be summarily convicted—if he was acquitted by a jury rather than a judge—but he is forced to submit to a new trial; if he is again acquitted, the process can continue ad infinitum. The Crown has infinite resources; the defendant is usually poor. The pressure on the defendant to bargain for a lower sentence rather than defend himself in court, which is usually great, becomes insupportable. It is this pressure which acts as the effective constraint; the Crown in fact rarely has occasion to make use of its appellate prerogative. More than 80 percent of persons charged with indictable offenses in Canadian courts plead guilty or are convicted by a judge. The judge has absolute discretion to deny a jury trial to any defendant subject to a term of less than five years' imprisonment if convicted—which includes more than 40 percent of those charged with indictable offenses—and, in any event, fewer than 2 percent so charged demand and receive a jury trial. This may, of course, merely reflect the perspicacity of law-enforcement officials in charging only those persons who are in fact guilty. But it must be reassuring to them to know that, in Canada, they can keep firing until they get their man. An American prosecutor gets only one shot; but in the United States, too, about 80 percent of persons actually brought to trial on felony charges are convicted. Double jeopardy isn't necessary for "law 'n' order." It probably isn't necessary either for "peace, order, and good government"—which is what the British North America Act seeks to secure for Canadians instead of "life, liberty, and the pursuit of happiness."

These fundamentally contrasting approaches to the process of criminal justice cannot be regarded as merely alternative ways of attacking similar problems, each equally appropriate to its own cultural context. They go to the very heart of the question of national identity; and Canadians, at least, recognize that they do. Many Canadians, especially ardent nationalists, have become disturbed about the infiltration of Canadian culture by American TV shows; and one of the complaints I have heard voiced most frequently concerns the fact that these programs subvert peace, order, and discipline among the young by leading Canadian kids to believe they have constitutional rights that even their elders cannot claim. Since the most vocal nationalists in Canada tend to be left-leaning intellectuals with a record of support for the political rights of minorities and poor people, it comes as a surprise to discover that they object to Canadian children learning the American conception of freedom even as a heuristic model from which to develop their own. This attitude is not, of course, confined to intellectuals; I recall especially two furious encounters I have had on the subject of the effect of American television police shows on Canadian youngsters: one with a municipal police officer whose duty and pleasure it was to visit the high schools in his community to sell students on the virtues of obedience to the law; the other with a university professor at a conference concerned precisely with the impact of American enterprise on Canadian culture. Both these men were distressed because American television police programs, though usually fanatically supportive of law 'n' order, still showed that bad guys, deplorable as this might be, had certain established rights: the right to be informed by the arresting officer at the time of arrest of the charges under which the arrest is being made; the right to make a phone call and obtain legal counsel before being interrogated; and later, should the case come to trial, the right to decline to answer on the grounds that the answers might be self-incriminating. The Criminal Code of Canada recognizes these problems, but does not deal with them by extending full guarantees to suspects and accused. The arresting officer, according to article 29 of the Criminal Code, must "give notice to the arrested person, where it is feasible to do so, of . . . the reason for the arrest; the Canada Evidence Act provides the equivalent of what in the United States is called "use immunity," which prevents the use of a witness's specific testimony as a basis for further charges against him—but does not preclude its being used as a key to searching out further evidence in support of these or other charges. Moreover, the Supreme Court of Canada has ruled that relevant evidence may be introduced by the Crown against a defendant even though that evidence was unlawfully obtained.

Both the professor and the policeman who spoke with me were distressed because young Canadians who watched American television were being misled into thinking they had such rights. Neither of them was at all disturbed because they *didn't* have these rights; they objected only to the fact that Canadian youth were being instilled with an alien and misleading view of social reality. When I suggested to the professor that it might be useful for young Canadians to learn that a social system *could* provide these rights and that they were therefore possible in principle, his rejoinder was that Canadians might have evolved their own equally effective safeguards of liberty if they had not been so constantly tempted by the American chimera. The police officer was less articulate, but when I asked him how many of the young people he had warned against believing they had the same rights as Americans, had ever asked him *why*, as Canadians, they did not possess such rights, he told me—I thought proudly —that none ever had.

Unlike Americans—and, for that matter, unlike the British, who have had their share of rebellions and revolutions, some of them glorious—Canadians as such have no tradition identifying government as the source of oppression.* They resisted the temptation to join the American revolution; and their loyalty to the Crown was indeed reinforced by the flight of loyalists northward from the revolting colonies. Neither William Lyon Mackenzie nor Louis-Joseph Papineau, the Ontario and Quebec leaders, respectively, of the unsuccessful Rebellion of 1837, sought or envisoned independence from Britain; their objectives were limited to greater local autonomy, to be insured by election rather than appointment of executive officials, and the vesting of the power to fund their salaries in legislative appropriation rather than in the provisions of a civil list, so that these officials could no longer be paid by the Crown from year to year directly from public funds without the need for legislative appropriation.

Canadians like to boast that their system of government is not encumbered by separation of powers like the American government, though it is not always clear what they mean by

---

*Just two Canadian public officials have ever been murdered. One of these of course, was Pierre Laporte, Quebec provincial minister of labor and immigration, who was slain in 1970 by his Quebec terrorist captors. The other was D'Arcy McGee, a member of the first federal Parliament, who had been an Irish nationalist but became a supporter of confederation and the British Empire after moving to Canada. He attempted to discourage the Fenian raids then being organized among Irish immigrants in Ontario and was shot to death in front of his Ottawa home in 1868 by another Irish nationalist who had remained militant.

that. They are scandalized by any hint that a minister of the Crown may have attempted to influence a judge to support a policy of his ministry, but not by the fact that their judicial system provides so few procedural safeguards—after all, the Crown and the Bench are collaborators in the administration of the Queen's justice. Parliament as a whole has few investigative powers and does not have the authority to subpoena witnesses and examine them under oath. It can establish committees, like American congressional committees, which may or may not possess such powers according to their particular orders of reference. So-called royal commissions, usually limited to the investigation of particular events or situations, do possess such powers. But they, too, are really created by ministerial or cabinet action and cannot therefore usually be established if their investigations seem likely to embarrass the government. Persons appointed to serve on them are often associated with the abuses they must investigate, which doubtless qualifies them as experts but also makes them, in a broad sense, judges in their own cause. Royal commissions hold their most sensitive meetings *in camera* and report directly to the government in office, which has no obligation to release the report, though it may be under considerable pressure to do so. If, nevertheless, a commission of inquiry should venture into areas in which the government finds its attentions unwelcome, a minister of the Crown may, at his discretion, withhold any document or evidence from it—or, indeed, from any court whatever—if he deems that producing it might jeopardize not only "national security" but "Privy Council secrets" or even "federal-provincial relations." Section 41-2 of the Federal Court Act grants him this power and also denies any court, even the Supreme Court of Canada, the right to question his decision or examine the evidence for that purpose. Under Canadian law, President Nixon's claim of the right to withhold tapes under executive privilege could never have been tested in court.

The Supreme Court of Canada has very limited powers. It cannot declare any act of Parliament unconstitutional except on the grounds that it is an invasion of an area, like education, that the British North America Act reserves to provincial rather than federal jurisdiction. The Court does not reject legislation on the grounds that it conflicts with the established rights of Canadians. Canadians possess no such entrenched rights; what Parliament has granted, Parliament may take away. The Canadian Bill of Rights was not even adopted until 1960. Copies of it on simulated parchment have since enjoyed widespread display in classrooms and other public places. Its impact—so far barely observable—and its limitations will be discussed in detail in chapter 4.

The Bill of Rights has done nothing to limit the extraordinary powers of search and seizure possessed by the Crown, which remain much as they were at the time the American Founding Fathers sought to insure, by means of the Fourth Amendment, that authorities in the United States would never possess such powers. The Criminal Code of Canada requires that the officer conducting the search obtain a warrant based upon reasonable cause—and carry it with him and produce it "when feasible"— but Canadian courts, including the Supreme Court of Canada, have held that illegally obtained evidence may be used against the accused, whose only remedy, even if acquitted, is a civil suit against the officers who committed the illegal search. Moreover, writs of assistance are still valid in Canada, and some two hundred of them are in force at the time of writing. These are issued to individual members of the Royal Canadian Mounted Police as well as to specified members of the investigative staffs of narcotics, customs, and income tax bureaus on demand and remain valid as long as the agent is a member of the force. He may use the writ of assistance to search any premises in his jurisdiction in which he has reasonable cause to believe evidence of wrongdoing is to be found—and, essentially, he is the sole judge of what is reasonable. While the writ is not transferable, the presence of one officer who has such a writ suffices to legitimate the activities of any search party of any size. There is no nonsense about "particularly describing the . . . thing to be seized," as the Fourth Amendment puts it; RCMP raiding parties don't just ransack residences looking for pot; they carry off truckloads of filing cabinets from respectable but suspect business firms. What is remarkable is that, despite their extraordinary powers, they sometimes, like the FBI, break into buildings and seize documents illegally. They need have no fear that, by doing so, they will destroy the evidentiary value of materials obtained.

Seizures so broad in scope, even when lawfully conducted, can of course be used to put an adversary out of business by destroying his records and work place and denying him access to them, regardless of the course or outcome of any subsequent litigation. Early in 1978, for example, the Toronto police made especially sinister use of the power of seizure in a raid on the offices of *The Body Politic*, Toronto's long-established militant gay newspaper. The cause of the raid was ostensibly a complaint against an article considering the value as well as the dangers of love relationships between men and young boys. Whether the article was scurrilous or not, it was most certainly offensive to a community that achieved the notable distinction of being the only large metropolitan center in North America to ban Louis Malle's film *Pretty Baby*, in which the pedophilia discussed (though never depicted on screen) was at least heterosexual. But the evidence that a document is pornographic must, in the nature of the case, be derived from the material itself. To support the charges brought against *The Body Politic*, only the publication could have been pertinent, and that could have been obtained at a newsstand. The police, however, seized most of the files in the office, including the subscription lists, without which the paper could not function and which could have had no bearing on the charges of obscenity—though the knowledge that the police had seized them could, of course, serve to intimidate subscribers. Efforts by attorneys of *The Body Politic* to obtain a court order requiring the return of these lists were unavailing; the court permitted the Crown to retain the lists, requiring only that a photocopy be returned to the paper so that it could continue to function. When, in due course, the defendants were acquitted of all charges by the judge at their trial, Attorney General McMurtry refused to return the seized documents on the grounds that the Crown intended to appeal against the acquittal, as it has since done.

Canadian law provides no effective defense against such inquisitorial raids. What is clearly absent from Canadian political consciousness, though salient in the American, is the conviction that the state and its apparatus are the natural enemies of freedom. It is not that Americans are more tolerant—Larry Flynt, shot in the bowels by a citizen crusader against pornography too eager to await the judgment of the courts, could attest to that—or that on their record Americans have been consistently devoted to liberty. The American system, though, places less trust in authorities and tends to preserve liberty, at least formally, even when the people are negligent or hostile.

The differences, of course, may easily be exaggerated; they may also be decreasing, primarily due to restrictive decisions by the U.S. Supreme Court. A recent decision, for example, permits the introduction of illegally obtained evidence in grand jury proceedings. Since President Roosevelt's day, American presidents have increasingly relied on executive orders to bypass Congress; like Canadian orders-in-council, these have the force of law. But orders-in-council that would be subject to judicial nullification as unconstitutional, or to attack by Congress as offensive to their special constituencies if promulgated as American executive orders, prevail quite easily in Canada. For example, under the new Immigration Act of 1977, the cabinet has the power to order the deportation of any alien, however long domiciled in Canada, without giving any reason and with no possibility of any appeal to the courts.

While the Congress can also include in legislation restrictions on the judicial review of its provisions, this legislation itself is subject to review on constitutional grounds, as it would not be in Canada. Congress could attack the principle of judicial review of legislation directly—that is, by passing legislation restricting the power of the courts generally; this would be much harder for the courts to deal with in the absence of specific constitutional entrenchment, especially since they could hardly appear as plaintiffs. But the consequence would be a major constitutional crisis. Indeed, in the United States at present, it is the courts rather than the executive which seem to be most active in restricting access to information, both by imposing "gag" rules about reporting current trials and by the use of contempt citations to force reporters to reveal their sources. This also happens in Canada, where a member of the Ontario Parliament was recently imprisoned for a week for refusing to say who had revealed information to him that had led to accusations of corruption in a medical insurance program. Canadian law governing reporting of pending or current trials is, in general, so restrictive that "gag" rules are hardly necessary in individual cases. Members of Canadian trial juries are forbidden by law *ever* to reveal the discussions that led to their verdicts.

American constitutional guarantees, however, are less securely grounded formally than Americans usually suppose. The power of judicial review is not established by—in fact is not considered in—the United States Constitution. The Constitution does, of course, establish the Supreme Court as the court of final resort in a judiciary designed to function independently of the executive and legislative branches—though its justices are appointed by the executive with the advice and consent of the Senate. But the Constitution nowhere specifically provides the Supreme Court with the power to rule legislation or executive orders invalid on constitutional grounds. The power of judicial review is merely implied by the doctrine of separation of powers; in the absence of that doctrine, the Supreme Court of Canada has never developed to the stature of its American counterpart. (Canada's parental model, Great Britain, does not even have a supreme court; the ultimate power of appeal in any lawsuit rests with the Law Lords—in effect, a standing committee of the House of Lords that consents to hear certain appeals unsystematically on a case-by-case basis, but has no power to rule on the validity of the statutes under which the cases have been brought.) But the power of the U.S. Supreme Court to make such rulings is not constitutionally entrenched either, and this fact has undoubtedly made the Court more cautious and conservative in challenging legislation than it might have been.

Americans cannot, then, rely on the Constitution to protect their liberties as fully as they may like to think. But the mere fact that Americans believe they have these rights and can count on them, while Canadians do not and are not greatly concerned about the lack, makes for a much greater sense of openness south of the border and a freer play of expression, much of it of redeeming social value. The differences are sometimes subtle and occasionally gross, but they are observable in most areas of human activity whose results are likely to be affected strongly by their participants' conviction—or lack of it—that spontaneous and unauthorized action by themselves or others is likely to get them somewhere.

It is hard to imagine any area of human activity that would not be so influenced to some degree. But the effects are especially notable in the arts and in the economy, though where the economy is concerned they are far more difficult to distinguish from among the complex factors influencing economic events. With respect to the arts, Canada seems to excel particularly in those forms with least potential for subversion. Canadian ballet has been recognized for years throughout the world; there are at least three established companies of first rank, and they are not only competent but reasonably innovative artistically—certainly compared to Russia, if not to the United States or England. This seems astonishing in a nation of less than 25 million people, addicted to hockey and the RCMP Musical Ride. But ballet, though highly expressive, is also the art that provides least opportunity for spontaneity or improvisation; it is governed by an elaborate system of conventions and requires lifelong discipline of its practitioners. As a form, moreover, it is peculiarly unsuited to exploring the implications of human experience, just as it is peculiarly suited to expressing the feelings associated with such experience. The story of *Petrouchka*, for example, could easily have been used in a fairly typical Chaplin film. But Stravinsky and Fokine have a very different effect on hearts and minds; and the medium, in any case, is not cinematic. Statements made through ballet can be and at best are *universal*, in the sense of expressing a feeling any human being might share; but they cannot be *general* social propositions, which is one reason why socialist realism seems like something totally different from ballet even when danced by technically perfect companies. Moreover, the medium really is the message, as one of Canada's greatest living poets insists, and the context of ballet is still anti-mass and arty. The form, in its North American context, is inherently counterrevolutionary. *The Ecstasy of Rita Joe* is bitter and moving, though self-conscious commmentary in ballet form on the oppression of native people in Canada today; and it has been and is generally admired by Canadian devotees of the arts. But it does not tell a person who attends it nearly as much about the plight of the Indian as the sight of the audience getting off on its own liberalism for no more than the price of admission tells him about the role of the arts in Canada. Should any poor Indians chance to attend a performance of *The Ecstacy of Rita Joe*, they had best be prepared, for their own comfort and safety, to take part in a panel discussion afterward. Otherwise, the minister of Indian affairs and northern development might just revoke their band status.

The more literary and dramatic arts have rather special problems in Canada, however. Government support, at least until budgets began to tighten seriously during 1977, has not been one of them. The level of support provided through such publicly funded but self-governing bodies as the Canada Council has been remarkably generous; the United States government has been niggardly by comparison and the National Endowments for the Humanities and for the Arts, latecomers to the field. Wealthy Canadians, it must also be noted, have not set up private—or, more precisely, extragovernmental—foundations on the scale of the Ford Foundation, though the use of private foundations to hold voting stock in and thus retain control of family corporations while reducing the burden of taxation is accepted practice in both countries. But on the whole the arts, including literature, cannot be said to have languished for lack of funding.

Nor has censorship been an exceptionally severe problem in Canada. The arts might be livelier, as in many ways they are in Hungary or Russia, if it were more overt. Canada, however, is a country much more given to self-censorship. So, of course, is the United States; the *apparatchiki* of the creative arts are exceedingly trendy in both nations. Most artists and writers have been willing enough, as they have had to be at most times and places, to suit their work to the patronage available in order to flourish. But there are more options in the United States, and more acceptance of social strife as an inevitable and even grimly enjoyable part of life and of history.

Of course, it is easier to enjoy books and movies about civil war in a society haunted by the memory rather than the prospect of such a conflict. But the enjoyment of conflict is not a part of the Canadian tradition as it is of the American. The Can-

adian West was won, not by massacre and military conquest—
though there were, of course, regrettable incidents from time to
time—but by the Northwest Mounted Police as they were then
called, moving ahead of the colonists to inform the native people of their lack of civil rights. Law and order, Canadian school-
books say, preceded the settlement of the frontier, begging the
question of whose law and order it was.

There is not really much pluralism in Canada. Sociologist
John Porter, whose best-known book is called *The Vertical
Mosaic*, intends by his title to contrast the structure of Canadian society, in which he believes the cultural identities of each
contributing ethnic group are preserved, with the American
melting pot. But the metaphor is somewhat misleading. It is
true that Toronto seems an especially cosmopolitan city because
of its great variety of ethnic neighborhoods, colorful and distinctive. But one thing that keeps them colorful and distinctive
is the fact that they appear quaint, unassimilated, in a way that
attests to the impregnability of the Anglo-Scottish matrix in
which each colorful chip is appropriately affixed. There is no diversity of norms accepted by the white Protestant majority; the
social attitude toward ethnicity that actually prevails is conveyed
more accurately by a large billboard posted in stations throughout the Toronto subway system in the summer of 1977. It
showed a multitude of boys and girls of about the same age and
different characteristically ethnic features, each clad in a shirt
with a maple-leaf design. The caption: "From different pasts; a
common future." I never saw one of these defaced, which made
me nostalgic for New York.

Where there is a genuine respect for pluralism and diversity
and a considerable, albeit still inequitable, distribution of political and economic power among a variety of social groups with
different values and cultural standards, there is much more for
the arts to feed on, both for support and for content; while conflict itself serves as a major and enduring theme. The Anglo-
French conflict has provided Canadian literature with such a
theme, though it has been far better and more widely exploited
by Francophones than by Anglophones, with notable exceptions
such as Hugh MacLennan's *Two Solitudes* and, of course, the
work of Mordecai Richler, who, being Jewish, is exempt from

full membership in either group. More recently, growing and intense resentment of American cultural domination has presented another popular theme for Canadian writers, with impressive results in the hands of Margaret Atwood and regrettable ones in those of Richard Rohmer.

The weakness of genuine pluralism in Canada means, however, that work which takes the unpopular side of a cultural controversy runs a greater risk than in the United States of sinking without a trace, instead of being preserved by the sponsorship of an intransigent minority until it becomes publicized by its opponents and attackers. The Canadian media usually treat opposition to the established position on any issue as a breach of taste, to be ignored or ridiculed but not seriously refuted. One of the most flagrant examples of this behavior in recent years has been the treatment accorded the efforts of the Greenpeace Foundation to halt—or even to observe—the annual seal hunt and attendant slaughter of infant seals in international waters off the coast of Newfoundland. Not only has the government of Canada effectively closed the area to observers, including California Congressman Leo J. Ryan (later slain in the Jonestown massacre in Guyana), to whom it had previously given reluctant permission to undertake the costly and inconvenient journey; it also funded, through the Canada Council, an exceedingly odd satirical review presented by a well-known Newfoundland theatrical group called the Mummers and entitled "They Club Seals, Don't They?" The review was advertised as presenting the "other side" of the seal-hunt issue and protrayed the protesters as vulgar intruders motivated by greed, drawing exorbitant salaries from their supposedly philanthropic effort, and grossly disrespectful of Newfoundland folkways. CBC news reports of the arrests and harassment of Greenpeace and other observers in 1978 and 1979 avoided showing the carnage itself, as they had done in previous years, and unquestioningly repeated official statements.

There is much social conflict in Canada, of course; but to be recognized, it must be ritualized. What is suppressed is spontaneity rather than opposition—anything out of control. The Canadian system of government could not tolerate members of Parliament taking it upon themselves to oppose—or support—measures regardless of their party affiliation, just because they or their constituents actually think they should. During the current struggle between Quebec and the rest of Canada, Liberal members of Parliament in Ottawa have frequently been called upon and threatened with discipline by the party if they do not support measures they have reason to believe are hostile to the interests of their own constituencies. The clearest example of this is the pressure put on Quebec Liberal MPs in Ottawa to support federal tax policies regarding Quebec introduced by federal Minister of Finance Jean Chrétien in May 1978—policies the Assemblée Nationale in Quebec City, with a substantial Liberal membership, had unanimously condemned.

In Parliament, opposition is not left to interest groups or mavericks. Leader of the Opposition is an official title for a salaried office, held by the elected head of the party with the largest minority of seats in Parliament—the official, and loyal, Opposition. Social and political conflict in Canada can be very acrimonious, but the struggle tends to be as stilted and agonizingly slow as classical Japanese Noh drama—though in style, Parliament more closely approximates Kabuki. The result of this institutionalization of opposition is to deprive it of an authentic viewpoint of its own, since it is obliged, in the very act of expressing itself, to declare its basic acceptance of what it opposes. Opposition that is openly, even though not violently, hostile is pointedly ignored as naughty and made to stand in a corner till it mends its manners. One of the opponents of the minister of finance in the tax controversy just mentioned called the minister a liar; the Speaker of the House expelled him from his seat in the House of Commons for a day, the usual penalty for a breach of Parliamentary etiquette—but nobody considered the question of whether M. Chrétien had in fact lied, and about an issue of some importance.

Substantial and disruptive issues are not fought out in Canada; when they are reported they are immediately buried under questions of deference and etiquette. Sometimes it can be seen happening in the course of a day, like one day in the spring of 1977 when the morning CBC news carried a report taken from a private working document of a parliamentary commission inquiring into the functioning of the Canadian Penitentiary Service, which had just been leaked to the press. The document alleged gross brutality and incompetence or worse against certain officials of Millhaven Penitentiary and accused specific individuals, including the director of the prison and local officials of the prison guards' union, of participating in the abuses detailed there. By noon, however, the news broadcasts had shifted their emphasis from the content of the document to the fact that it had been leaked without authorization—just like south of the border. By evening, the story had been eclipsed by the apparently more shocking fact that the prime minister had once again lost his temper in the House and had snapped at one of his parliamentary critics, "For Christ's sake, shut up!"

Attempts to probe deeply into the meaning of life in Canada—which is what the arts here, as elsewhere, are supposed at best to do—become curiously self-defeating. It's like expressing real and deep feelings in a commercially sponsored encounter-group session: the more authentic you are, the more you betray yourself and the more deeply ensnared you become in the artifice and corruption you're trying to expose. This happens in the United States, too; but the mechanism is different and the defeat is less overwhelming. True, you risk becoming a professional black, or gay, or hippy, or whatever; and thereafter your identity as a professional or even a celebrity may alienate you from the very group whose cause made you what you were. But at least the dominant society recognizes, and continues to recognize, that those groups are still there and have norms of their own; *they* are still out in the world trying to make it on their own terms. Furthermore, the rewards of self-betrayal are much higher and more freely negotiable in the United States—real money and power, for what they may be worth, which in American dollars can be a real temptation. In Canada, the top prize is cooptation: acceptance by the very club you are criticizing; which is not much of a basis for negotiation if you meant what you said in the first place. This, fundamentally, is why English Canada cannot begin to respond to the cultural demands of Quebec. What can one offer them, when they do not want to live like Albertans even if they could afford it?

Canadian society is in many respects far more tolerant than American. American society cannot, in fact, be very tolerant; there is nobody with the authority to do the tolerating. Instead, there are specific rights; but one must defend them against other contenders who claim the same rights but interpret them adversely. In a tolerant society a wide variety of points of view and life-styles may be accommodated precisely because they have so little status; a single, dominant set of standards and point of view have already been established.

The National Film Board of Canada, a government agency under the jurisdiction of the secretary of state for Canada, was established during World War II primarily as a propaganda agency and, in the beginning, a crude one. It quickly outgrew its origins and deservedly became respected throughout the world as a maker of original, sensitively conceived documentary films that often deal with the kind of topics termed "controversial." This is not surprising. Good documentary films are the ideal expression of the liberal, tolerant mind: concerned, judicious, ready even to concede that it is an important part of the problem and to criticize or condemn its own weaknesses—but *not* for one moment prepared to admit that the problem may not be what it thinks it is, or that someone else might have the right and the power to define the problem differently, or even to declare that there is no problem, only a drama and probably a tragedy. Much the same thing can be said of the Canadian Broadcasting Corporation as of the film board, but only insofar as productions of and by English Canadians are concerned. When French-Canadian talent is involved, real drama becomes possible, such as Michel Tremblay's *Les Belles Soeurs*, and Cam Hubert's *Dreamspeaker*, directed by the distinguished Québecois, Claude Jutra. The latter deals as uncompromisingly and heartrendingly with authority as the heart of darkness as anything I have ever seen on television. Neither of these productions is French; both originated in the Vancouver studios of the CBC and were presented in English. Hubert, whose real name is B. A. Cameron, is a British Columbian woman. Neither play, however, shows a trace of English didacticism. What Quebec contributes is the unalterable conviction, rare in English Canada, that secular authority is very much a protagonist in the drama rather than the source of the social and moral norms in whose light the events portrayed must be considered. No Quebecer who was not also an ardent federalist could believe that; if Sophocles had, he could hardly have written *Antigone*.

For, I believe, much the same reasons, the best Canadian commercial films originate from Quebec: *Mon Oncle Antoine*, *Wedding in White*, *Les Ordres*, and the American-made but faithful-to-Montreal *Apprenticeship of Duddy Kravitz*. An exception that proves the rule is *Outrageous!*, made in Toronto, in which homosexuality triumphant as the central theme provides the ironic detachment from WASPish norms ordinarily found in Quebec nationalism. A brilliant review of this film in *Canadian Forum*,* contrasting it with Margaret Gibson's book *The Butterfly Ward*, on which it is based, makes these observations:

> Although structured as fiction, the book was a blatant statement on mental health care and written from so flatly personal a viewpoint as to be almost a print documentary. Documentaries are, of course, the instrument of the official culture, which has drummed into our heads the notion that they are good for us. Thus the book was warmly, officially received in much the same spirit as C.B.C. specials on freight rates. "Poor Gibson," people seemed to say "she's to be pitied for being different—and applauded for calling our attention to this difference so that we can bring our records up to date."

> A similar reception would have been given the movie had [the director and scriptwriter] made the film anything remotely resembling a documentary. If the film had treated Russell [the homosexual hero] as an unfortunate aberration and McLaren [the schizophrenic heroine] as a sicko—had it, in short, been stimulating, informative and significant—the response would have been one of official gentility—and box office death. Instead, partly because he is himself gay, Benner treated them as perfectly legitimate people and got on with telling the story with polished dialogue and a minimum of facts. And this, I think, is what delighted (or at least surprised) an audience brought up to think of Canadian cinema as an endless series of docudramas.

> Here was a Canadian film based on the truth we all know but seldom see recorded rather than on the facts in the newspapers and one not remotely concerned with Prairie childhoods or the other circumstances by which the government, and those it has employed, try making art from tourist flakery. Here instead was a decidely unofficial film about the urban environment in which the majority of the population actually live. And one not mainly interested in social politics, as it so easily could have been. It is clear that Liza is naturally sane when left to her own devices and that she goes strange only when on drugs prescribed for her stability. It would have been simple to make a statement to the effect that Ontario's system of mental health treatment is insidious: that anyone can be committed on little

*December-January 1977-78, *57* (677), 65-66.

evidence, that class is the determining factor in who's considered normal and who's not. Such a statement is necessary, sure; but the point is that *Outrageous!* takes this for granted just as it assumes many other truths which a documentary would have tirelessly set about explaining.

One doesn't have to be gay to know that Toronto is probably the *underground* gay capital of North America. One just has to live on the outskirts of officialdom. One need not be very observant to know that most of what's culturally interesting in the place comes from the streets in which the gays, crazies, emigrés and other outcasts interact and go for the most part officially unnoticed.

The audience for *Outrageous!* knows this world or knows of it but seldom sees it reflected in the culture it buys. The glory of *Outrageous!*, it seems to me, is that it finally takes cognizance of the fact that whatever excitement there is in Toronto comes about in spite of the O'Keefe and the St. Lawrence Center, the C.B.C., the N.F.B. and the newspapers, not through them. The film doesn't boldly advance this viewpoint (for then it *would* be a closet documentary of sorts) any more than it peeps through the keyhole at supposed depravity and eccentricity. Rather it takes this world at face value, using it as background against which to tell a perfectly simple, straightforward tale.

The simple, straightforward tale is also a very sentimental one; all the gay characters who play significant roles in it have hearts of gold; only straight, authority figures like parents and doctors are nasty. The border is no problem either; in fact it proves to be a resource. Russell makes it big in the New York nightclub scene as a female impersonator and brings McLaren there to continue his care for her after the stillbirth of her baby precipitates a breakdown in which she insists that she, too, is dead. "You're not dead, Liza," Russell tells her in the most quoted line from the film: "You're alive and sick and living in New York like eight million other people!" Palpable wish-fulfillment. Try substituting "three" for "eight" and "Toronto" for "New York"; and it sure doesn't work.

For those Canadians who are neither gay, psychotic, or Québecois, creativity in the arts seems to come harder—harder than in many smaller and more oppressed nations that are further handicapped by the obscurity of their language. The basic problem, I would insist, is the inability of English Canada to express itself adequately on the relationship of man to authority—

surely one of the most basic issues with which the arts must deal. Sophocles, Shakespeare, Schiller, Dostoevski, Achebe, Joyce, Beckett, Melville, Conrad, Ibsen, Kafka, Yeats, Strindberg, Mann, Doris Lessing, Cortázar—all these have come to grips with this problem, at different times and in different languages, more often than not from a basically conservative position, for conservatism is not conformity. But I doubt that an Anglograph Canadian could write as seriously as these have done about the effect of authority on human behavior. The habit of deference is too ingrained in Canada; the dissident becomes either a victim or a plucky schoolboy, ready, finally, to resolve his dispute with authority by taking six of the best from the prefects. Louis Riel, John Brown's Canadian counterpart— the métis leader who was hanged in the Northwest Mounted Police barracks in Regina in 1885—is not really a hero in Canada. A modern statue of him has recently been somewhat incongruously erected, after great controversy, on the provincial capital grounds in Winnipeg; and a pseudodocumentary film about his life was finally released in April 1979. But no song asserts that *son âme marche toujours!* though recent Canadian history makes it reasonably clear that it does. He will never be *respected* in English Canada as Sacco and Vanzetti have come to be in the United States—though their English wasn't too good, either.

To treat seriously an outlaw, a revolutionary, or just a marginal antihero of the type Gene Hackman or Jack Nicholson usually play, the drama must to some extent accept, though it need not endorse, his point of view. It cannot, instead, treat him either as a social problem or as doomed by definition because he has no proper place in society; his antisocial or asocial quality cannot be portrayed as *inherently* pathetic and absurd. In Canadian novels and especially Canadian films, however, this is the way such characters usually are treated. It is hardly ever suggested that they themselves are not troubled by their marginality, except for the practical problems it creates, and are certainly not ashamed of it; that life is something they intend to live and, if possible, enjoy on their own terms. The characters in *Outrageous!*, however, do—which is what makes the film so exceptional.

Another 1977 film, *Why Shoot the Teacher?*, starring Bud

Cort as an amiable, ineffective, penniless beginning schoolteacher, is a much more representative example of the Canadian film genre. It was even more enthusiastically, and much less ambivalently, acclaimed by critics across the nation as evidence that Canadian filmmakers could make splendid, warm, nostalgic comedies. In this one, Cort borrows train fare from Ontario to the remote Saskatchewan village of Willowgreen to take the only job he could get in 1934, full of self-doubt and affection for his prospective pupils. Throughout the murderous winter in this inhospitable hamlet, which is depicted as realistically as the teacher and his pupils are sentimentalized, he is bullied both by the villagers, who pay him only scrip, and by his pupils, one of whom he finally forces himself to strap—though it is to the film's credit that the boy takes his beating in bad grace. At the end of a school year of almost unendurable hardship, Cort rushes from the one-room schoolhouse shouting, "I'm free! I'm free!" But the film ends with his return to teach in Willowgreen in 1935.

Why Shoot the Teacher? combines some curious discordancies of tone. The strength of the film is its portrayal of the nastiness, emptiness, and brutality of life in Willowgreen, precisely illustrating what Marx must have meant by "the idiocy of rural life." If Cort had played the teacher as a grown man forced by circumstances to share their lot as best he might, or even as a Chaplinesque little man who survives by resilience and guile, it might have been a great film. But he plays the role in just the opposite way, as a patsy. His failures are not efforts to sabotage the trap he is caught in; they do not imply that he is capable of rebellion, and whenever he tries to stand up for himself or what he believes in against community pressures, he fails miserably. It is quite inconceivable that Cort could simply say either to his recalcitrant older pupils or to the School Committee members who bully him, "Enough of this bullshit—you're wasting my life." There has to be a face-off, with Cort usually the loser except, finally, with his pupils.

Authority cannot be dealt with lightly in a Canadian film; it can be ridiculed, broadly, but not dismissed as unimportant. For this same reason, the teacher cannot be shown as capable of winning the genuine interest of his pupils by real competence.

Authority must be a problem for him, too; the film must show both him and his pupils broken in to serve it willingly. He is being fagged, hazed, by farmers instead of public school prefects, so that he will know in turn how to administer discipline. He, too, is a "new boy." The message, with the world and the blizzard howling continuously at the door, is that endurance and loyalty to the task set by authority come first, even when the task is futile or absurd and the authorities cheat you and abuse you. Only children, like the teacher and some of his pupils; comedians, like the village socialist, presented as a dolt in the very time and place that Canadian socialism was being born as an enduring political force; and the doomed, like an aging war bride who turns to Cort for support and love he is too respectable to give her and is ignominiously hauled away by her hateful and embittered husband—only these rebel, for rebellion cannot, must not, solve anything. To grow up means to accept, to come back for more of the same, next year. Come back, as the school-teacher says he did, at the end of the film, and reassume the position. If it is argued that the film is based on an autobiographical account—as it was—and must deal with events as they occurred, I would reply that cultures nevertheless reveal themselves by the events they choose to make legendary, and the values expressed in the legend. Lots of people traveled by train during the 1930s, and several of them rode their way right into the nostalgic films of the 1970s. Only three years after Max Braithwaite's abject journey on the Canadian National, young Miss Lillian Hellman entrained from the Gare de l'Est on a Berlin Express of the French National Railways, bound for Julia with $50,000 of serious political money hidden in her hat. She had her problems, then and in the rest of her life; but few of them seem to have been occasioned by an insufficiently critical attitude toward authority.

One Canadian author, at least, solved this problem boldly and successfully, if perhaps a little evasively: Marian Engel. We do not even have to worry about whether Bear is Anglophone, or consider his implications for national unity. Many critics from Northrop Frye on have emphasized the almost obsessive role played by the harshness of nature in Canadian literature, and certainly it looms large in Canadian life and legend. But I suspect that one reason for the prominence of man's struggle against the rigors of Nature as a theme in Canadian literature is not only that it is a valid, significant, and recurring aspect of Canadian experience, but that it is the only struggle that is ideologically acceptable. If it's Nature you're fighting, it's okay to be resourceful and competent; you don't have to parody your manhood like Bud Cort in *Why Shoot the Teacher?* It's okay to win, as Canadians clearly have—poor old Nature, poisoned unto the Arctic tundra with mercury, arsenic, and asbestos wastes, has poor prospects for victory, at least in the short run. Fighting Nature doesn't make you a rebel; Nature has enormous—indeed, lethal—power, but she has no authority at all. She is entitled to no deference, which means that it is sometimes possible for Canadians to think about her honestly and with genuine awe and respect.

2

Secrecy and Authority in Canadian Society

The governments of Canada—federal, provincial, and municipal —are among the most secretive of any democracy in the world. Like Great Britain, and unlike the United States, Canada has an Official Secrets Act making it an offense to transmit secret information to persons unauthorized to receive it, or to receive such information without authorization. The Official Secrets Act does not apply only, or even especially, to secrets allegedly related to national security. It applies to any information the government wishes to restrict. It could, for example, have been invoked against the distinguished Canadian journal of opinion and policy, the sixty-year-old *Canadian Forum*, which in November 1971 published an abridged version of the Gray Report, a theoretical but controversial government position paper on the effect of foreign ownership on the Canadian economy. The Liberal government of Mr. Trudeau had refused for some months either to release the report or to indicate when it proposed to do so; the Editorial Committee of the *Forum* simply took a calculated risk in what it held to be the public interest and got away with it—presumably permanently, though there is no statute of limitations on prosecution under the Criminal Code of Canada. The dam having been breached, the government did then issue the report, titled *Foreign Direct Investment in Canada*, in 1972. The Toronto *Sun* was less fortunate. On June 12, 1978, publisher Douglas Creighton and editor Peter Worthington were brought to trial under the Official Secrets Act, though charges were dropped some months later. The newspaper was charged with publishing portions of an internal RCMP document concerning possible Soviet espionage in Canada, quoted by an Opposition member of Parliament on the floor of the House in a statement in which he suggested that members of Canada's security forces were being too soft on the Russians; the document was offered to raise questions about why these forces were not acting on evidence they apparently possessed. For a few days after Mr. Cossit's statement in Parliament, the Canadian media were filled with titillating speculation about whether he, too, would be prosecuted; but the minister of justice resolved that question in a stern statement deploring the member's behavior but affirming the parliamentary privilege —which American congressmen also enjoy—which forbids members from being brought to judgment in any other place for statements made in the legislative assembly. During the parliamentary discussion of the impending prosecutions, former prime minister John Diefenbaker, who opposed them, pointed out that the secret document had in fact been officially distributed to at least fifty-eight government offices. Not quite a year later, the charges were quietly dropped. Meanwhile, before the *Sun* trial began, the Supreme Court of the United States handed down a verdict dismissing a case against an American newspaper that had been prosecuted for publishing restricted information that had been leaked to it. The government, the Court found, is responsible for maintaining discipline in its own house. It can proceed against officials who violate security regulations, if it can make a case against them; but it cannot look to the courts to protect it from its own indiscretions by abridging the First Amendment rights of the press.

The United States does, of course, have legislation designed to protect information it wants to keep secret for security reasons from being revealed even by persons who have come into possession of it perfectly lawfully and without getting it from any government source—even when they themselves are the source of the information. In May 1978, George I. Davida, an associate professor of electrical engineering and computer sciences at the University of Wisconsin, Milwaukee, was served with a secrecy order imposed by the U.S. Patent Office, forbidding him under threat of up to two years imprisonment and a $10,000 fine from publishing an apparently successful study designed to find ways of protecting the security of computer programs—a hot topic in these times of accelerating computer fraud. The research was not classified—the University of Wisconsin does not accept classified research contracts—and was publicly funded by a $90,000 grant the National Science Foundation awarded Mr. Davida in December 1977, while he was still a graduate student. But U.S. patent law permits the Patent Office to impose such secrecy orders at the request of any one of a dozen unidentified defense agencies, on patent applications for inventions or techniques that may contain information related to national security.

The University of Wisconsin protested this action vigorously and publicly as a violation of freedom of research, and the Department of Commerce rescinded the order within a fortnight. If it had not, and if Professor Davida had violated it and had been prosecuted, he would at least, in the United States, have been tried in open court. In Canada, Alexander Peter Treu, a German-born physicist and naturalized Canadian, was tried and convicted under the Official Secrets Act in a closed, secret trial held in Montreal in the spring of 1978. He was sentenced to two years' imprisonment. Treu had retained certain records of his own work on a classified NATO project after it had ended—records which, he declares, he was never told to surrender. Several years after the project had been concluded, the RCMP raided his home and seized the records, charging Treu with, among other things, not having guarded them properly, though they did not claim that anyone else had gained access to them. At about the same time, the United States government was conducting a public trial in Alexandria, Virginia, of an American, Ronald Humphrey, and a South Vietnamese, David Truong, on charges of espionage involving the transfer of documents that were undoubtedly classified, though of disputed value as objects of espionage. The two were convicted, for better or for worse, on six of the seven counts with which they were charged, in an adversary proceeding in open court. If the government had not wished to present the necessary evidence, or had found it embarrassing to proceed for any other reason as it did in the Ellsberg trial, it would have had to drop the case.*

Early in 1974 the Quebec Court of Appeals reversed Dr. Treu's conviction and acquitted him. In this case the Crown decided not to seek a second trial.

As dramatic as the *Sun* and Treu cases are, and as important as they are as evidence that the Official Secrets Act is not some arcane and archaic provision of Canadian law but a very active one, these cases are less revealing of the process of secrecy in action than the issues that have arisen, and continue to arise, in connection with a totally different matter. In May 1978, attorneys for the solicitor general went before the Supreme Court of Canada to plead that the Quebec Provincial Commission of Inquiry into the conduct of the Royal Canadian Mounted Police be foreclosed because, among other reasons, its director, Jean Keable, had allegedly violated the Official Secrets Act in revealing information about the force's activities which he and his staff had obtained in examining prospective witnesses—information the solicitor general refused to disclose. M. Keable has not been charged with an offense under the act, but if he should be,

---

*One of the counts under which Mr. Humphrey and Mr. Truong were convicted does, however, have a sinister potential for creating by judicial precedent the equivalent of a freedom of information act, which would probably be judged unconstitutional if directly enacted by legislation. This danger has been explicitly discussed by political columnist Anthony Lewis on the op-ed page of the *New York Times*, Monday, June 19, 1978:

The two men were charged—and convicted—under Section 641 of the Federal criminal code, which makes it a crime to steal Government property. What was the property? The Justice Department said it was information, and Judge Albert V. Bryan Jr. followed that view of the law when he charged the jury.

"Information may be government property," the judge said, "apart from the document or the sheets of paper themselves." Thus it does not matter if the original government document remains in the files. Anyone who copies it or makes notes from it without official approval has still stolen "property."

For advocates of secrecy, the beauty of that legal theory is that it applies no matter what kind of government information is involved. National security need not have a thing to do with it. . . .

In short, the government property theory of information would give this country an Official Secrets Act. It would be potentially as devastating to the press and public knowledge as Britain's (or Canada's) much-criticized secrecy law.

neither the relevance to his inquiry of the material disclosed nor the fact that it constituted evidence of possible crime by the RCMP against the people of Quebec—whose rights, as a provincial official, he is obligated to preserve—would constitute a defense. This commission was established by the government of Quebec early in the fall of 1977 to look into the circumstances of the illegal entry at the Agence de Presse-Libre de Québec; as the ramifications of that affair became clearer, the government expanded its mandate to authorize investigation of any wrongful police activity in the province of Quebec. Since the dominant police presence in the province was the RCMP, itself an arm of the federal solicitor general's office and responsible for political surveillance and "dirty tricks" in Canada, a nation-shaking confrontation, if not a constitutional crisis, became inevitable.

It is with reference to the activities of the Royal Canadian Mounted Police and, particularly, the question of whether the most oppressive of those actions were undertaken with the knowledge or indeed at the behest of the solicitor general at the time, that the issue of governmental secrecy in Canada has finally become salient. Theoretically, of course, this should make little or no difference, since the Canadian government functions under the doctrine of ministerial responsibility; a cabinet minister is accountable for the behavior of the agencies and personnel under his jurisdiction whether he knows what they are doing or not. But, in fact, Canadian officials try as zealously as American officials to preserve what came to be called, during Watergate, their "deniability." This would ordinarily be much easier for them than for Americans, because of their extensive legal authority to conceal. But the Canadian federal system is vulnerable to one source of conflict to which the American federal system has gradually developed substantial immunity, through the devolution since the American Civil War of the doctrine of states' rights. These have not entirely ceased to exist, of course, but there is no longer any question that, in the United States, federal jurisdiction and certainly the U.S. Constitution is paramount. In Canada, as I have already indicated, the Constitution is only partly a written document; but the part that *is* written down— the British North America Act—is most specific in designating which spheres of authority are provincial and which federal.

Questions of jurisdiction still arise and are sent on to the Supreme Court of Canada for resolution, but these are either novel or borderline cases. The customary divisions between federal and provincial authority have become clearly established.

Sections 91 and 92 of the British North America Act provide for a rather curious separation of functions. The Criminal Code and procedure in criminal cases are established by Parliament. But "the Administration of Justice in the Province" is a provincial responsibility. This means that the responsibility for criminal investigations and the decision to prosecute under the Criminal Code of Canada, which is federal, are made by the office of the provincial attorney general, not by the federal minister of justice, and certainly not by the solicitor general, whose office has essentially housekeeping functions—though the houses it keeps, which include the RCMP and the Penitentiary Service, are not exactly open houses. Since provincial process is specifically excluded from the authority of the Canadian Bill of Rights, pretrial proceedings are not governed even by its rather meager provisions; and the fact that investigation and prosecution are defined as provincial responsibilities may even serve to strengthen the powers of the federal government.

Ordinarily, assignment of the responsibility to prosecute criminal cases to the provinces has few observable consequences. In Canada, as in the United States, provincial politics are bush league compared to federal politics, and Canadian politicians are normally, like American politicians, ambitious. The provincial governments are proving grounds for figures with national aspirations, and provincial premiers and their subordinates are unlikely to refuse to cooperate with the federal government, much less to adopt policies that threaten it deeply. This is not quite as true in Canada as in the United States, both because the provinces do retain relatively more powers than do American states, and because two smaller Canadian parties, the mildly socialist New Democratic Party and the highly conservative Social Credit Party, elect members to Parliament and also occasionally win provincial elections and form provincial governments. But these parties, too, have national aspirations.

Provincial governments frequently—indeed, routinely—squabble with the federal government about policies that affect them financially and sometimes even prevail. Ottawa was not happy about the so-called nationalization—really provincialization—of the largely American-owned potash mines in Saskatchewan a few years ago, for example, but could not prevent it. But provincial governments rarely challenge the Government of Canada on issues that question its integrity, or threaten to reveal that it has far less than was supposed.

Of course, under really bizarre circumstances—if the government of a province fell into the hands of a political party indigenous to that province; a party which not only has no national aspirations but hopes to lead the province right out of the nation; a party many of whose leaders were arrested in the middle of the night and detained incommunicado under the War Measures Act, and who believe, with some evidence, that the federal government used its police power in a criminal conspiracy to keep them from gaining office—under those highly exceptional circumstances, the provincial government might be tempted to use its investigative powers rather more boldly than usual.

In March 1976, an officer of the RCMP, Robert Samson, was convicted of an attempt to blow up the home of a wealthy and highly respected Jewish merchant in Montreal—an attempt so inept that Samson himself sustained minor but conspicuous injuries that led to his arrest. The crime seemed both brutal and senseless,* and led the judge who sentenced Samson to seven years' imprisonment—a term he is now serving—to berate him severely for actions inappropriate, as the judge thought, to a police officer. Samson, goaded beyond endurance, blurted out in open court that they were not that unusual, and asserted that he, himself, had taken part in a break-in at the offices of the Agence de Presse-Libre de Québec on October 6, 1972. So had his superior, Donald Cobb, the regional specialist for dirty tricks for the RCMP, and members of the Quebec provincial and Montreal city policy forces—there were, in this event, no unresolved

---

*Samson has continued to refuse to explain his crime. The most frequently suggested hypothesis is that this was one of several atrocities of which Quebec separatists were to be falsely accused; if so, this plot has not been publicly established.

problems of cooperation among the several levels of government. None of these had a warrant; but they rifled and seized documents which, as the story unfolded, appeared to have been taken to hamper efforts to provide legal defense funds for Quebec separatists.

The documents seized from Agence de Presse-Libre were destroyed. But on January 9, 1973, the RCMP broke into the offices of the Parti Québecois itself, again without a judicial warrant, and removed various documents, including membership lists, which it photographed and returned surreptitiously. The Parti Québecois, then as now, was a perfectly legal, established political power which, within four years, was to sweep the provincial Liberal government of Robert Bourassa from office; Bourassa himself lost his seat in the election of November 15, 1976. But the Liberal governments in both Quebec City and Ottawa apparently regarded the Parti Québecois as a band of desperate men against whom any measures were justified. Just what, and how extensive, these measures were has been a principal object of investigation by the Quebec Commission of Inquiry directed by Jean Keable who, as I have mentioned, has been named as a possible violater of the Official Secrets Act. The Keable investigation has been forestalled pending a decision by the Supreme Court of Canada, which heard the case in May 1978, on the right of the province of Quebec to conduct an investigation into the conduct of a federal agency, however unlawful it may have been. It has recently resumed hearings on a limited basis.

No one has yet been prosecuted for the break-in at the headquarters of the Parti Québecois, nor for any of many other apparently illegal actions about which evidence emerged, over the strenuous opposition of lawyers from the solicitor general's office, during the sessions of the Keable commission.

For four years, nothing was done about the break-in at Agence de Presse-Libre either. The Quebec minister of justice under the Liberal government, Jerome Choquette—who became famous for his unremitting prosecution of Henry Morgentaler— denied any involvement by the police when officials of the Agence complained. Their registered letter of complaint to then solicitor general Jean-Pierre Goyer was never even acknowledged;

Goyer denied having received it but later, in 1979, admitted that he had decided not to respond to it—on advice from the RCMP. Then, finally, legal action began to be taken by the province. The highest-ranking official of each of the three police agencies who had actually taken part in the break-in pleaded guilty to unlawful entry when the case came to trial in May 1977. Their guilty plea of course foreclosed the possibility that any testimony would be taken at the trial itself. Judge Robert Vincent, after accepting their plea, discharged them unconditionally without a stain on their records and publicly commented on the nobility of their motives, though it is not clear how he had established what these motives had been. That evening's newscasts reported that Superintendent Cobb was already back on the job, though they didn't say what he was working on.

This should have ended the matter; but by this time the Parti Québecois had been in office for six months; the Quebec provincial police, which under the previous Liberal government of Robert Bourassa had cooperated with the RCMP when asked without troubling too much about its agenda, were now responsible to the new adversary. The Keable commission was established, and drew blood and made headlines from the start. If its revelation of the scope of RCMP activities in Quebec—which included a monotonous series of break-ins and more bizarre crimes like the burning of a barn in which some suspected potential terrorists were planning to meet with American Black Panthers—came as no astonishment to Pèquiste insiders, it certainly made headlines throughout the rest of Canada. Judging from letters to members of Parliament and phone calls to the CBC—neither, to be sure, likely to yield an unbiased sample of public opinion—the headlines were arousing widespread public support in Anglophone Canada.

The position of the solicitor general, at that time Francis Fox, was therefore less conflict-ridden than it appeared. Nominally the minister accountable for any misconduct by the Royal Canadian Mounted Police, who are under the jurisdiction of his office, he also had the practical problem of defending them. The break-in at the Agence de Presse-Libre had occurred just before Jean-Pierre Goyer left the office of solicitor general, while that at Parti Québecois headquarters took place during the administration of the latter's successor (and Fox's predecessor) Warren Allmand. Under the parliamentary system, ministerial responsibility is enforced by persistent questioning from Opposition members during the Question Period which concludes daily sessions of Parliament. But Mr. Fox could not be held responsible for, or even questioned about, the actions of his predecessors. The Speaker of the House, James A. Jerome, had earlier established a general rule that no former cabinet minister could be questioned about events that had occurred during his term of office, so that even though M. Goyer and Mr. Allmand were still sitting members of Parliament—and, indeed, still held cabinet posts—they could not be questioned either. Moreover, it appeared that those—primarily Opposition—members of Parliament who reacted indignantly to the information being made public by the Keable commission were getting in trouble with their constituents for not defending the quasi-sacred RCMP. The Canadian press expressed fears that Canada was about to be shaken by what it called a Mountie-gate; instead, the Canadian public and, increasingly, even Parliament seemed to be responding like the townsfolk of Titipu at the end of the first act of *The Mikado*, drowning out the embarrassing revelations of the disaffected Katisha in a frenzied chorus of nonsense syllables that kept them from hearing what they didn't want to hear.

All three solicitors general, past and present, made public statements denying any personal knowledge of the misconduct, if any, of the RCMP while under their nominal control. Such statements, however, even if true, are no defense under the doctrine of ministerial responsibility. Meanwhile, less sweeping investigations of RCMP activities in other provinces were revealing highly questionable activities in many different areas of Canadian life. An inquiry conducted by Mr. Justice James H. Laycraft of the Alberta Supreme Court, which began as an investigation of the possible financial manipulations in Alberta of an American carnival company, Royal American Shows—and of possible irregularities by the RCMP and the Edmonton city police in the actions already taken against them—brought to light a secret agreement, officially known as a "memorandum of understanding between the solicitor general and the Department of National Revenue," under which the RCMP have access to income tax returns filed in Canada, although the confidentiality of such returns is guaranteed by Canadian law. The attorney general of Alberta was not informed of the agreement, but found that the evidence seized by the Edmonton police in their initial action against Royal American Shows had been seized from them in turn on July 29, 1975, by the federal Department of Revenue, which feared that Royal American Shows might succeed in getting the original search warrant quashed and the evidence returned to it. The Laycraft inquiry was then established to sort out the confusion about who was doing what to whom; but by fall of 1977, its operations faltered in the face of heavy stonewalling by both the RCMP and the Department of National Revenue. The original target, Royal American Shows, appears for the time, at least, to have gotten lost in the shuffle. Access to income tax returns of individuals suspected by the RCMP of having some connection with "organized crime" has been nationwide, however. Moreover, in April 1979, the Supreme Court of Canada ruled that the RCMP could proceed to try, in secret and before its own private tribunal, the officer who responded to the summons of the Laycraft inquiry and disobeyed orders by testifying before it. He may be imprisoned for a year.

Similarly, investigative reporting—understandably a rarity in Canada—conducted by the news services of the Canadian Broadcasting Corporation revealed that the RCMP had been opening and copying private first-class mail under a program called "Operation Cathedral." Canadian postal regulations, which are even stricter than American, make no provision whatever for this sort of interception of domestic mail. On November 9, 1977, Francis Fox confirmed in the House of Commons that such acts had taken place since 1956 (later testimony has suggested that the RCMP has been opening other people's mail in Canada for at least forty years); then, later in the day at a Liberal Party meeting in his riding near Montreal, Fox condemned the actions of the CBC as "irresponsible" and suggested that its budget be cut by the federal government. A cabinet meeting apparently hastily convened the next morning immediately issued a statement that Fox's recommendation did not represent government policy, and Fox himself said that his statement had been meant rhetorically, rather than literally.

If it still appeared that the Canadian public was unlikely to declare a Mountie-gate, it was equally clear that the RCMP had been, and doubtless still were, riding off rather unmusically in all directions. The solicitor general, for his part, seemed to define his ministerial responsibility as defending their flank and his own rather than getting them back into the corral. On June 17, 1977, responding to Opposition criticism in the House of Commons aroused by Judge Vincent's unconditional discharge of the officers who plead guilty to the Agence de Presse-Libre break-in, Fox had refused to consider appointing a commission of inquiry into the activities of the RCMP; but he did promise to cooperate with an investigation which Premier René Lévesque of Quebec had just promised to establish, in order to cast "as much light as possible on the rather inelegant operation." This, of course, referred to the formation of the Keable commission; but far from cooperating with it, Fox did all he could, until his own precipitate resignation from office, to obstruct it and close it down—though compared to his successor, Jean-Jacques Blais, Fox was a model of explicit candor. He refused to honor the commission's subpoenas for documents and made repeated attempts to have the inquiry disbanded as unconstitutional. Three of his appeals were turned down at successive levels of the Quebec courts; the fourth, at the next highest level, did stay the inquiry pending an appeal to the Supreme Court of Canada, which has now ruled that the inquiry may continue under greatly restricted terms of reference. Had the solicitor general failed to halt the work of the Keable commission, he could still obstruct its investigations by invoking the Federal Court Act in response to its subpoenas. This act empowers the solicitor general to withhold from any court or inquiry any document whose publication he deems prejudicial to: (1) national security; (2) the security of Privy Council secrets; or (3) federal-provincial relations. Since the Privy Council includes all persons who have *ever* been members of the cabinet in any government, however long departed, the Federal Court Act empowers the solicitor general to compel anyone who has ever held a cabinet post to carry secrets with him to the grave or, in the case of an ardent spiritualist like the late William Lyon Mackenzie King, to guard them even there.

Despite the reluctance of the groundswell of Canadian public opinion to expand into a breaker on which Jean Keable could hang ten, there was enough criticism in the media to suggest that Something Must Be Done. What Mr. Fox did, in July 1977, was to announce that the commissioner of the Royal Canadian Mounted Police had himself requested that a royal commission be set up to investigate the activities of the RCMP, and a three-man commission was appointed under the chairmanship of Mr. Justice David C. McDonald of the Supreme Court of Alberta. Like American congressional committees, the McDonald commission has the power to subpoena documents and witnesses and to examine witnesses under oath. It holds its sessions *in camera* or in open hearings, at its own discretion. Its members and essential staff are cleared to receive documents restricted under the Official Secrets Act, so that evidence cannot be withheld from the commission by invoking this legislation; though the commission is not free to reveal the evidence so collected, it can make public any recommendations it wishes, and it cannot be required to report anything it chooses to withhold.

From the outset serious questions have been raised in the press and the House of Commons about the effectiveness and impartiality of the McDonald commission; and, indeed, about its basic purpose. Royal commissions of inquiry are a classic Canadian solution to the problem of public scandal, and they often do a thorough and vigorous job of exploring the problems that lie within their mandate. They are nevertheless widely recognized as highly effective devices for seeing that nothing is done about the situations they are established to investigate. They take years to complete their work, and the ordinary legal processes that might otherwise be invoked are usually suspended until they make their report. Jean-Jacques Blais, as solicitor general, affirmed that no prosecutions of RCMP personnel would be undertaken until the commission makes its final report, which is not expected until 1982—though an ordinary citizen against whom there was as much evidence of illegal entry, unauthorized and literally unwarranted seizure of private documents, intimidation and harassment of prospective informants, and, in one case at least, arson, would long since have been brought to trial. Whatever the intent, the first and most obviously predictable consequence of the formation of the McDonald commission has been to confer at least temporary immunity to prosecution on the RCMP officers and officials involved. The decision whether or not to prosecute in any individual case is, moreover, constitutionally the responsibility of the attorney general of the province in which the offense is alleged to have taken place rather than of the federal government, which is why the Keable commission could be established in the first place. Solicitor General Fox, and his successor M. Blais, however, consistently used the existence of the McDonald commission as part of their justification for refusing to cooperate with the Keable commission and, indeed, to get it adjourned. The net effect of the McDonald commission, so far, has been to protect those it is investigating from the normal operations of Canadian criminal law. It may recommend prosecutions, in its report, but by that time witnesses will be hard to assemble and their memories much impaired. It may also make no such recommendations. Critics of its operation, including the Canadian Civil Liberties Association, have publicly protested that the policy of the government in delaying prosecution in these cases cannot but undermine respect for law itself; but the argument has proved unpersuasive.

Neither the composition of the McDonald commission nor its functioning during its first year of operation have done much to establish its impartiality. The chairman is a respected justice of the Alberta Supreme Court; he is also a former president of the Alberta Liberal Party and for many years has been a close friend of Prime Minister Trudeau—as the president of the party organization in Canada's richest and probably least Liberal province ought to be. Both the other members of the commission, Guy Gilbert and Donald Rickerd, are reported by CBC news to be close friends and associates of Francis Fox; one is a Liberal politician. There are no members of the Opposition on the commission, and requests by the Progressive-Conservative Party for representation before it by a minority counsel empowered to examine witnesses—normal procedure for American congressional committees, as viewers of the Senate Watergate committee will remember—were refused by the McDonald commission. A similar request by the Canadian Civil Liberties Association to have counsel present to represent the public interest was also refused on the grounds that this function was the responsibility of the commission's own legal staff.

There is certainly no question that this *is*, indeed, the responsibility of the commission's legal staff; but there is rather more doubt that it is discharging this responsibility with as much zeal as the CCLA would have brought to the task. It took the commission five months to begin public hearings after it was created. The delay has been attributed to the extremely complete security checks required for service on a commission from which Solicitor General Fox had promised that no document requested would be withheld—a promise to which he repeatedly reverted in publicly justifying his refusals to supply these same documents to the Keable commission or the Laycraft inquiry. Since the standards for what sorts of attitudes and what kind of past record form the basis for deeming a Canadian a security risk are determined largely through the security practices of the RCMP itself, it is difficult to see how persons who had been critical of such practices in the past could qualify for service on the commission, even if an effort were made to avoid bias in favor of or against the RCMP.

At any rate, hearings were begun in December 1977. Initially there was widespread criticism in the press of the apparently desultory questioning of RCMP witnesses by commission counsel and of the alacrity with which the commissioners acceded to requests by counsel for the RCMP to continue *in camera* hearings that were becoming embarrassing; the public hearings often seemed more like public platforms from which the RCMP might make its case than sessions devoted to investigating its conduct. In recent months, this criticism has abated; and there have been some complaints from RCMP counsel about the vigor with which their clients are being questioned. My own subjective impression, based entirely on press and television coverage of the hearings, is that most of the adverse testimony taken in public hearings so far—that is, up to mid-June 1978—has come from witnesses sufficiently aggrieved by personal experiences at the hands of the RCMP that they could hardly have been restrained from making their complaints publicly anyway, now that the RCMP is in the spotlight. On June 14, 1978, the commission voted two to one to allow counsel for the RCMP to cross-examine hostile witnesses about their personal political and/or criminal backgrounds in order to establish credibility—a ruling that led one witness to protest indignantly that it was apparently he, rather than the RCMP, who was on trial. The commission has so far been notably reluctant to introduce into the public record documentary evidence pertaining to possible government complicity in the alleged misdeeds. On one occasion when commission counsel referred to a letter from a high official of Revenue Canada giving his opinion that the RCMP's use of tax records was probably unlawful, counsel for the solicitor general protested sharply that this was unfair, because the solicitor general had not released the document.

Critics concerned about the possible bias of the McDonald commission have been quick to insist that they have no doubts about and do not intend to question the personal integrity of its members. They may all be as honest as the day is long—and in Edmonton, in June, the sun does not set until nearly midnight and rises again quite early—but their personal integrity is not the issue. For in view of the use the federal government is making of it—and it is a creature of that government—it constitutes by its very existence a legalized obstruction of justice. Suppose, for comparison, that all prosecution with reference to Watergate had been postponed, awaiting the report of the Senate committee. The very course of American letters, as well as American history, during the last quarter of the century would have been different. The fact that he appeared as a witness before the Senate committee already convicted and sentenced, with nothing more to gain by lying, provided the basis for John Dean's credibility when nothing else could have. The McDonald commission, however zealously it may be investigating the actions of the RCMP, is nevertheless shielding it from the laws of Canada. No other accused await the generalized findings of a royal commission before the Crown even considers whether or not a case should be brought against them. Mr. Creighton and Mr. Worthington found themselves before the courts within a few weeks of the Toronto *Sun*'s publication of the putatively secret documents concerning Soviet espionage in Canada. No other accused are represented by counsel before an august tribunal whose responsibilities include determining whether existing evidence against them may, as a matter of public policy, be considered in determining whether a crime has been committed, let alone offered in court if a trial should be held.

Any protection the McDonald commission may be affording the RCMP is, however, incidental to its central function, which is protecting the legitimacy of the Government of Canada. Indeed, as many members of Parliament have pointed out, the information that has by now been brought to light—so far as it applies to the RCMP itself—is not really all that scandalous or shocking. It is only scandalous or shocking to people who cherish a highly idealized set of notions about what police actually do in a modern state. Every kind of malfeasance that has yet been alleged against the RCMP has likewise been committed by the FBI, the CIA, and other security forces, federal or local, in the United States, usually on a much larger scale as befits the comparative sizes of the two countries. I do not recall that the FBI ever burned down a barn; but I do remember that a false report of a fire alarm was used to gain entry to Fred Hampton's Chicago apartment, when no probable cause for issuance of a warrant could be found, so that he and other Black Panthers could be gunned down by Chicago police. Mail openings, improper access to medical records, recruitments of informers by harassment and intimidation, the improper use of income-tax information— all these have been commonplaces of North American police practice. On other continents, where citizens have not even the illusion of constitutional rights, things are usually even worse.

The same parallels are to be found with respect to the tendency of responsible government officials to make statements that turn out to be misleading. One of the most annoying recurrent themes, during the first few months of the Mountie-gate— that is, the last five months of 1977—were the successive assurances that Solicitor General Fox passed on from his immediate subordinates that each incident brought to light by the Keable commission or the CBC was an isolated example reflecting the political temper of the October crisis—though that had occurred in October 1970—rather than established policies, authorized or at least countenanced by the commissioner of the RCMP or the solicitor general. The power of the Honorable Francis Fox

to reassure the people of Canada on this and other points seems
not to have been impaired by the revelation, previously mentioned, of his early forgery—an act committed while he was already a member of Parliament though not yet of the cabinet.
The Canadian press, especially in comparison to that in the
United States, tends to play down scandalous events in the private lives of public figures if these are not related to their official
duties; and though Fox was obliged to resign from the cabinet
and absented himself briefly from Parliament, he retained his
seat and his career prospects; the press and the prime minister,
though deploring the incident, defined it as a sexual misdeed and
expressed a hope that so promising a young public servant would
not be lost to his country forever for this reason. Such forbear-
ance is in itself commendable—Premier René Lévesque bene-
fited greatly from this tradition when no large scandal was made
of the fact that, a few nights after his electoral triumph, he ran
over and killed a man apparently lying dead drunk in a Montreal
street under circumstances that would clearly have left him
blameless except that he was not wearing glasses at the time, as
his driver's license required. Most reports did not even mention
that his mistress of many years' faithful standing—they were finally married in 1979—was a passenger in the car at the time.
Neither adultery nor lack of vision is usually regarded as a serious impediment to the career of a political leader; forgery, however, especially under a political system that provides so few opportunities for the independent verification of official statements, might be thought a more troublesome tendency.

But what has been so repugnant is precisely the strenuous
and, under the circumstances, bizarre and frantic efforts to convince the media and the public that the RCMP was not engaged
in any officially sponsored program of political repression in
Quebec and that responsible officials had not been aware of the
incidents that were reported until the news broke publicly. What
if it was? What if they were? That wouldn't make Canada Russia;
it would merely indicate once again that governments in power,
when they feel that power threatened, will do almost anything
they think required to retain it. Under its infamous Cointelpro
program, the FBI did worse to Puerto Rican nationalist groups
and to the impotent Socialist Workers' Party than the RCMP has

been accused of doing to the Parti Québecois, which represented a real threat—not because there is any evidence that it is inclined to terrorism, but because there was a lot of evidence, not totally misleading, that it might win.

The fact that abuses very similar to those that have occurred in Canada take place in the United States does not, of course, imply that abuses of police power are tolerable, or that they may be viewed with complacency in either country—or anywhere else. My point has to do with an altogether different issue. What I find most disturbing about the situation in Canada is the astonishment at what should by now be regarded as a political commonplace as well as a serious abuse of power, and the widespread acceptance that the accused, if they occupy or have once occupied positions of power, may never be required to disclose fully just how they used that power. The presumption that they act and have always acted in the public interest, and that the public interest would be threatened if its nature and the means by which it is defined and defended were closely scrutinized— that presumption is, under the Canadian system, overriding. The shock of knowing how their country is really run would, it is assumed, be too great for Canadians to bear; and they, themselves, avert their eyes when the authorities tell them to.

But there is, or should be, nothing shocking about discovering that police have abused civil liberties and that their responsible superiors have helped them conceal their misdeeds. It is no more shocking than the discovery that the family dog has messed on the rug; it can't be permitted to continue, and you may have to smack the animal with a newspaper to teach it to quit, or get rid of it if it simply can't be trained. But the disclosure of the mess and how it happened does not bring discredit on the household; indeed, this is the only way to get it cleaned up. Sweeping it under the rug and accepting it as evidence that the dog is zealous in defending the security of the home will, however, soon make the house uninhabitable. The householders may also help to forestall such domestic tragedies if they learn to detect, by its usually stiff and pompous gait, when the creature is really full of shit, and turn it out before it gets a chance to do further damage.

In a democracy, civil authority is strengthened—though

an incumbent government may be imperiled—by accepting the fact and the consequences of its own wrongdoing. The presidency is not endangered by the discovery that the president is indeed a crook—at least, not as much as it would be by the refusal to deal openly with the possibility that he might be. The Canadian way, however, seems rather to be to attempt *ex post facto* to legitimize those questionable actions of authority that have become public, even at the price of grossly distorting the institutions within which they function—and this really does endanger such freedom as the Canadian system of government provides. After the break-ins could no longer be denied, the solicitor general and his staff argued repeatedly that there might, after all, have been no crime committed, because the police had not had any criminal intent or *mens rea*. Any first-year law student knows, however—and any citizen had better know, if he hopes to stay out of jail—that *mens rea* has nothing to do with malice. It does not refer to intent to do harm or commit an act that one believes to be wrong. If you intend to do something which is in fact forbidden by law—whether you know it is or not—you have criminal intent, or *mens rea*, under law. If the police on that fateful night in Montreal had, while pursuing a pickpocket down a slippery street, accidentally slipped on the pavement and crashed through the windows of the offices of the Agence de Presse-Libre they would indeed not have been guilty of unlawful entry, since they had not intended to break their way in. But since they *had* intended to break in, the fact that they believed their motives for doing so were noble, and that the solicitor general and prime minister would agree with them, cannot absolve them of criminal intent. From watching Mr. Fox advance this argument on television and his Parliamentary private secretary—also, of course, a member of Parliament—do so at a public debate on the matter held at the Dalhousie University Law School, I would infer that they did not expect the argument to be accepted but wished to impress their audiences simply by the *chutzpah* with which they advanced it, with their determination not to admit they were wrong no matter how absurd or illogical their position might be.

With reference to the interception of mail, there is simply no room for denial that such action is against Canadian law. The prime minister has taken the position that the illegality of these actions is for the courts to determine; but, if they do determine that such mail openings are illegal, the law must be changed to permit them. The Liberal government had, in fact, presented the first draft of legislation permitting the solicitor general— not even a magistrate—to authorize such mail-tapping as he now can do with telephones, before it was swept from office. Allan Lawrence, solicitor general in the present Progressive-Conservative government, has followed up the campaign promises of his leader, Joe Clark, by asserting that legislation authorizing the RCMP to open mail in suspected criminal cases will be given "highest priority" when Parliament reconvenes in October 1979.

Prime Minister Trudeau's basic approach to the problem of police misconduct was made clear in the following excerpt from his press conference held in Ottawa on December 9, 1977, and later reported in the *Toronto Globe and Mail*:

> I have attempted to make it quite clear that the policy of this Government and, I believe the previous governments in this country, has been that they, indeed—the politicians who form the Government— should be kept in ignorance of the day-to-day operations of the police force and the security force. I repeat that is not a view that is held by all democracies, but it is our view, and it is one we stand by.
> Therefore, in this particular case, it is not a matter of pleading ignorance as an excuse. It is a matter of stating, as a principle, that the particular minister of the day should not have a right to know what the police are doing constantly in their investigative practices, in what they are looking at, and what they are looking for, and in the way in which they are doing it.
>
> Maybe there are some people in this country who think that should be changed. I have argued the contrary. I have even some concern with the amendment now in the Official Secrets Act which, as I was answering the question earlier, permits the Solicitor-General to know at least some aspects of the day-to-day operations, that of wiretapping. I am even uneasy about that, but as an exception, I can live with it.
>
> I would be much concerned if ignorance of that particular investigative operation by the security police were extended to all their operations and, if, indeed, the Minister were to know and, therefore, be held responsible for a lot of things taking place under the name of security or criminal investigation.
>
> That is our position. It is not one of pleading ignorance to defend

the Government. It is one of keeping the Government's nose out of the operations of the police force, at whatever level of government.

On the criminal law side, the protections we have against abuse are not with the government, they are with the courts.

Since the police and security forces are arms for the execution of government policy, this would appear to be an argument not just for separation of powers, but for political schizophrenia —and, certainly, for not letting your left hand know what your right hand is doing. Since, as the events in Quebec and the fate of the Keable commission have so far demonstrated, the citizen who feels that he has been the object of police abuse cannot gain access to the evidence needed to appeal to the courts and cannot usually induce the Crown to prosecute, the remedy envisioned by Mr. Trudeau is valueless. And since the doctrine of ministerial responsibility does not admit ministerial ignorance as an extenuating factor, it is difficult to see on what philosophy of government his policy is ultimately based.

The Canadian Civil Liberties Association has attacked Trudeau's position—and especially his suggestion that, if the security forces have been systematically doing what the law forbids, the law should be changed—as grossly conducive to disrespect for the law and therefore unacceptable. But this response, though correct, seems to me dangerously inadequate as well as characteristically Canadian. It assumes that respect for the law is a Good Thing and that there cannot be too much of it. But Canadians already have too much of it, and to lose some would probably do the country good. The problem is that Canadians think the RCMP *is* the law—a view that the prime minister's position tends to encourage. But this view, as far as the average Canadian is concerned, is as correct, empirically, as any simple statement about law and society in Canada can be.

Canadian society is deficient, not in respect for law but in respect for liberty. And the fundamental function of secrecy in Canadian governmental practice is not concealment but the cultivation of docility. Governments rarely succeed in concealing anything important from their enemies—one of the most enlightening ironies of the Ellsberg case in the United States was its revelation that the Hanoi government knew—and had complained about—nearly everything in the Pentagon Papers that the government was calling a secret. Governments are somewhat more successful in keeping information from their own citizens, but only from those citizens who would rather not risk knowing. We found this out about the Germans after the Nazis were defeated. What Official Secrets Acts do is legitimate the ignorance of the citizens and convince them that they have no right to know what their governors tell them it intends to conceal. If their gaze happens to fall on father in his nakedness, they will be struck dumb; and it serves them right.

Peace, order, and good government in Canada depend ultimately on the deep acquiescence of the people in the idea that they have no inalienable rights; ultimately, the final decision rests with the cabinet. Instead, they have ombudsmen, negotiators whose responsibility is to present the citizen's case to the authorities and try to get him a better deal. Every province in Canada has one except the very smallest, Prince Edward Island— where everybody knows everybody else, anyway; the federal government is now setting up such an office for the nation. Some ombudsmen, like that for Ontario, carry on extensive and heavily budgeted programs with large and fairly aggressive professional staffs; others seem to do little but cool out complaints. Even the Penitentiary Service had an ombudsperson until she resigned in June 1978. But it is of the essence of their position that ombudsmen have no authority, while their clients, as such, are not asserting rights—if they were, they would turn to lawyers instead.

In practice, this system has worked quite well, perhaps as well as or better than an adversary system based on well-defined rights would have. But it depends, for its success, on a citizenry ready finally to accept Papa's definition of the situation and Papa's resolution of it, and persuaded, ultimately, that it has no right to ask questions that probe into matters it has been told are not its concern. In return, the government must in fact be somewhat responsive, and adept at offering fairly satisfactory compromises and services that ease crisis situations. The Canadian government has been good at this—better, in my view, than the American. It usually seems to be trying to help. When it has the resources to do it.

Inflation and unemployment impose severe strains on any social system, however, and especially on one that depends essentially on patronage and gentility to reduce conflict. The latter tend to vanish with the money, especially as competition becomes keener. The difficulties are compounded by the peculiarities of British-derived ethnocentricity. In view of the experience of Arabs and Jews, for example, I would not argue that the British have the most ethnocentric culture in the world. But they and their Canadian descendants seem to have more difficulty taking other people seriously; they are amused or annoyed by the woggishness or froggishness of lesser, non-Anglophone breeds, and basically consider it something these people do just to be cute or annoying, and to get their own way, like bad children—even people whose separate-but-equal status has been guaranteed by the terms of confederation. The material produced by both the Keable and the McDonald commissions indicates that the RCMP did not really think that the people of Quebec had any distinctive political rights at all; and they seemed to have assumed that the Québecois would agree with them.

Minorities need rights badly in Canada; and they don't have them. Neither do Anglophones, but they have privileges; and besides, the minorities, being voluble, aggressive, and uncouth in breeding, make trouble about it. Neither Henry Morgentaler nor Alexander Peter Treu have behaved quite like gentlemen about being sentenced to prison in unique and peculiar judicial proceedings. Each, too, has drawn champions, at least with respect to apparent violations of their civil rights, from among established Canadian conservatives—notably, in both cases, former prime minister Diefenbaker, who was also an ardent admirer of the RCMP. Canada is changing, and the fact that, beginning with the October crisis and the Morgentaler case, Canada has been racked by a mounting series of scandals about violations of what would be civil liberties if Canadians had them, is not a sign of mounting oppression, but of mounting discord about an oppressive system that went unchallenged for more than a century. Parliament is now even considering a Freedom of Information Act, and Nova Scotia has passed one, though both these acts in their present form leave the citizen with no right to appeal beyond an adverse decision of the cabinet minister in whose area of responsibility the inquiry falls. Both acts also carry long lists of exclusions and have been criticized for this reason as legitimating and therefore facilitating concealment while giving the citizen no rights he didn't have before. They cannot be called steps in the right direction; but they are indications that governments are beginning to realize that refusal to answer no longer suffices to embarrass and silence inquiry. It should also, in all fairness, be pointed out that the American Freedom of Information Act, if adopted in Canada, would provide no information either, because Congress, thoughtfully enough, excluded the operations of the legislative branch of government from its provisions. It would not, therefore, be applicable to Parliament or its agencies, and under a Parliamentary system of government with departments disposed under the authority of cabinet members drawn from Parliament, that covers everything. My point is not that it would be impossible to draft freedom of information legislation that would actually work in Canada if it could be passed, but that the American example provides no precedent for supposing that a legislature can be induced to pass laws that make its own operations an open book.

Despite the difficulties, the thrust toward greater openness in Canadian government proceedings is now too strong to be ignored. It came primarily from the Progressive-Conservative opposition; whether the PC government now in power will fulfill its commitment to freedom of information, we shall soon see. One might have expected a little better performance from the government of Pierre Trudeau, who came to power as a professed civil libertarian on the basis of a record as minister of justice under Lester Pearson that thoroughly supported his claim. He still declares himself to be a civil libertarian; but the record now makes it clear that what he supports is really a kind of Marcusian repressive tolerance. He *does* believe that human freedom and variety are good in themselves—Trudeau is no redneck or good old boy, and his frequent angry outbursts of gutter language in Parliament are as refreshing as his subsequent denials of them are embarrassing. But he also believes and has often affirmed that, in a serious conflict between the requirements of the state and the rights of the individual, the rights of the state come first. Trudeau himself is, of course, a Quebecer and a Francophone, though an undetectably bilingual one; and the French—as Tom Paine discovered when a brief term in the Chambre des Députés nearly led him to the guillotine—have never taken the Rights of Man quite as seriously as the British —or the Americans.

The failure of the prime minister to defend either the civil liberties of Quebecers or the rights of Canadians to discover how these liberties, and those of other Canadians, have been abused, is in this context understandable if inexcusable. But if the Liberal Party has allowed itself to become the apologist for and perhaps the designer of policies that ought to have been anathema to it and to its leader, the New Democratic Party, too, has been less explicitly vocal than might have been expected in defense of freedom and individual rights. The nominally socialist NDP finds itself in the curious and perhaps enviable position of having a better voting record by far than its rhetoric would lead voters to expect—at least on civil liberties. Only the NDP, for example, voted against the invocation of the War Measures Act in the October crisis, and it did so solidly though not quite unanimously. No member of either of the two major parties opposed it—though Robert Stanfield, then the leader of the Opposition, subsequently apologized for not having done so, and one member of his Progressive-Conservative Party did vote against extending the authority of the act when its term had expired. The negative vote came from David MacDonald, a young clergyman from Prince Edward Island now serving as secretary of state for cultural affairs, who is an outspoken supporter of civil liberties—by Canadian standards at least. The NDP almost always votes in support of freedom; but it doesn't talk about it much, perhaps in deference to the distaste many of its working class good-buddy supporters feel for freedom in the abstract. But it may also be that the NDP votes for political freedom and freedom of information in Canada because to do so is to attack the existing fortress of privilege, rather than because of a fundamental commitment to liberty per se. Several provinces have had NDP governments in the past—though only Saskatchewan, whose NDP premier strongly opposes extension of the federal Bill of Rights to cover provincial legal process, does so at pres-

ent. Many aspects of human freedom fall under provincial jurisdiction. In this respect, the NDP governments have not made a
consistent difference.

The effective spokesmen for civil liberty in Canada are concentrated at present within the ranks of the Progressive-Conservative Party, though it would surely be an error to assume that
the converse statement was true and that most articulate Progressive-Conservatives are champions of individual rights. It
would also be naive not to recognize that this position has been
easier for the party out of power to take. Freedom of information is more appealing politically if the secrets to be disclosed
are those of an opposition that has been in power for twenty-five
years. Nevertheless, that is where the champions are to be found:
David MacDonald, whom I have already mentioned; to a lesser
degree, Flora MacDonald, now minister of external affairs, who
aroused a great deal of interest and some hope by contesting the
leadership of the Progressive-Conservatives during their last leadership convention and making recent statements deploring the
secret trial of Alexander Peter Treu. Most impressive of all is
Gerald Baldwin, longtime PC member for West Peace River, Alberta, and a most insistent supporter of an effective Freedom of
Information Act for Canada, who agreed to join the group of
counsel defending Dr. Treu during his appeal—an action that
would make him privy to the secret proceedings and, though it
will not legally empower him to reveal them, provide him with a
firm basis for questioning in Parliament the operation of the Official Secrets Act.

So the cause of openness in government is not hopeless in
Canada; but the prospects are not good, either. The most formidable stumblingblock is the absolute unwillingness of the government to grant the existence of any unalienable rights that it
may never legitimately transgress. Pressed by political events, it
grants minister's permits for otherwise forbidden actions; grants
special, controlled access to otherwise forbidden documents;
and, above all, appoints august bodies—themselves sworn to
secrecy—from whom nothing, or hardly anything, is to be withheld, with instructions to study the problem again and report
by 1984. What it does not do is establish the right of its citizens
to embarrass it without its consent and establish due process by

which this may be accomplished. It responds to its people, up to a point, but it always keeps the last word. Not just the present government; not just the federal government. Later in the spring of 1978, a private member's bill—that is, a bill without party sponsorship—which had been introduced by a member of the Ontario provincial Parliament acting on his own, achieved overwhelming support from both sides of the House during second reading, a very rare occurrence in Canadian politics. The next step would have brought the bill to the floor for final reading, possible minor amendments, and a vote at which it would probably have passed, considering the support it had received thus far. The bill would have granted very limited—but *specific*—language rights to the Francophone minority in Ontario. At present, it enjoys no such rights except those pertaining to federal business provided by federal law. This bill would have extended these rights to certain areas such as education and other provincial services in regions of the province where a large proportion of Francophones live. In these regions, the province already provides some such services, but it has no obligation to do so—it merely responds to existing political reality as it perceives it. The federal government had, of course, no voice in this provincial legislation but was known to favor it enthusiastically as a contribution toward national unity.

The legislation would have had no effect at all on life in most of Ontario, where seldom is heard an offensive French word. But much of Ontario is rabidly xenophobic, and a horror story entitled *Bilingual Today; French Tomorrow* has become a paperback bestseller. Premier Bill Davis, a Progressive-Conservative, refused to permit the bill to come to a vote by denying it a place on the Order Paper, or agenda—that is, he vetoed it in advance. It would, he said, have given Ontario Francophones nothing the government was not already showing its willingness to provide them. Why introduce the chill of formal guarantees when things were already being worked out by friendly negotiation? Only a few months before, a Francophone Ontario businessman charged with fraud who demanded that his trial be conducted in French under the impression that this right *was* guaranteed him, was informed that the province did not have enough bilingual judges and jurors to meet such a commitment and, in any case, could not afford the expense of preparing to try him in French when it was now ready to try him in English. He should have complained sooner, when something might have been arranged; but even at this late date the province was prepared to offer him simultaneous translation. This is the kind of flexibility the premier prefers to retain, instead of having his hands tied by legislative enactments. And it is only fair to note that M. Filion, when he was finally brought to trial—in English —was acquitted. His Anglophone co-defendants were convicted.

Canadians who believe that they have certain guaranteed basic rights and attempt to assert them against the government are quickly disabused of this notion, whether it concerns the right to freedom of access to information or to a trial in either of the government's official languages. For this reason, and in a rather sinister sense, the Canadian Civil Liberties Association may even be naive when it argues that to treat the RCMP and the officials responsible for its actions as if they were above the law can only lead to contempt for lawful authority. Most people are not such philosophers. The practical message, and quite possibly the one the government means to convey, is: "The Government of Canada *is* the law; and don't think that because the law protects us from you, it also protects you from us. If you think you were taught that in school, you surely must have forgotten what school was really like."

3

The Punishment Industry

On October 21, 1976, the solicitor general of Canada, whose department has jurisdiction over the Canadian penitentiary system, moved that Parliament's Standing Committee on Justice and Legal Affairs inquire into the functioning of that system. He may have gotten more than he expected. His motion was accepted, and on October 26, a Subcommittee on the Penitentiary System in Canada, composed of thirteen members of Parliament drawn from all four of Canada's federal political parties, was established. According to its report, which was tabled early in the summer of 1977, "(24) it held 72 formal hearings with 407 witnesses in 225 hours of recorded sessions, and spent more than double that time in informal hearings. It heard witnesses *in camera*. Some were so terrified of reprisals that they had to be sneaked into the hearings without being seen by officers or inmates. Not only prisoners, but also staff members were threatened by a few hoodlums among the guards. In one case, in order to get an officer before the Sub-Committee, subpoena power had to be used. . . ." More than 2,000 inmates and staff in seventeen Canadian institutions, including all seven maximum-security penitentiaries, were interviewed. The committee also visited a selection of American prisons for comparative purposes.

Its report was unanimous, for "(20) if there were to be cures, we knew we would have to return to Parliament with a unanimous report. The Sub-Committee Members set aside party politics completely and immediately went to work as a team." The first of its sixty-five recommendations asserts: "A crisis exists in the Canadian penitentiary system. It can be met only by the immediate implementation of large-scale reforms. It is imperative that the Solicitor General act immediately on this Report as a matter of the utmost urgency." Indeed, the subcommittee felt so strongly on this point that it asked that its term be extended so that it might continue to monitor the solicitor general's response, instead of being discharged, as is customary, after its final report had been received. The solicitor general, Francis Fox, refused.

Canadians have many reasons for national pride—more, perhaps, than they give themselves credit for in their more defensively nationalistic moods—and one of these, certainly, is the clarity, forthrightness, and depth occasionally found in official documents. Though *double entendre* is required by law of publications of the Government of Canada, obscurity and obfuscation are usually avoided. While investigating committees are often less than candid in their public reports, and may have been denied access to much information that would have been pertinent to their work but embarrassing to the government, what they do have to say can be impressively direct and unequivocal. The MacGuigan Report (as I shall hereafter call *The Report of the Sub-Committee on the Penitentiary System in Canada*, after its chairman Mark MacGuigan, Liberal member of Parliament for the riding of Windsor-Walkerville, directly across the river from Detroit) is a model of strength and clarity. Something must have been sacrificed in the interests of unanimity, but it is hard to imagine what.

This does not, of course, mean that even the most compelling reports are likely to result in constructive and effective action to remedy the ills they consider. Abuses, in Canada and elsewhere, occur less through malign neglect than because they reflect established and significant political realities. This is especially true of recommendations for reform of the penal system, for reasons we shall consider, though some of them are self-evident. The excellent recommendations on work programs and industrial workshops made by a Royal Commission on Penitentiaries in 1914 have never been implemented in Canada; nor have those made by the 1938 Archambault Royal Commission, the 1969 Ouimet Report on Corrections, or the 1972 Swackhamer Report on the Kingston Riot resulted in any fundamental change. Nothing perceptible has yet been done in response to the MacGuigan Report; and one of its strongest recommendations has, as we shall see, become remarkably unpersuasive in view of the material brought to light by the recent and continuing investigations of the Royal Canadian Mounted Police.

Canada incarcerates about 9,000 adults in federal institutions at any given time—a higher proportion of its population than in any other Western democracy, though the United States jails a larger total proportion of its population when inmates of state prisons are included. In Canada, any convict sentenced to two years or more is committed to a federal institution; about 10,000 shorter-term offenders—though the statistics are not very reliable—are held in provincial or municipal institutions. There are eight times as many prisoners in state prisons as in federal prisons in the United States, and there is no systematic difference in the severity of the crimes for which they have been convicted.

Though local institutions that hold minor offenders are usually more squalid and barren of resources even than federal penitentiaries, the MacGuigan Report is concerned only with the federal system, describing conditions observed there and attempting to explain how they could have arisen and to suggest possible remedies. Its approach and tone are conservative, especially in its attitude toward authority. Indeed, the report begins with the following statement: "To sum up the totality of needs of the Canadian penitentiary system, as we have observed them, in a single word may seem as hazardous as it is ambitious. However, we believe the word 'discipline' says it all." The Subcommittee on the Penitentiary System in Canada immediately went on to explain that not merely the prisoners but the guards and indeed the entire penal establishment require discipline. This is more than a "system of rules"; it is "an order imposed on behaviour for a purpose. It may be externally imposed, but internally imposed self-discipline is ultimately more important." The report remains consistent with its introduction throughout; it is no less conservative for being both sharply critical of the existing penitentiary system and humane in its attitude toward convicts. It never questions, for example, that the penitentiary system has a purpose which might be served if order were successfully imposed on behavior; and it certainly does not question that such a purpose might be useful and constructive—this, it assumes. But by the MacGuigan committee's own account, the penitentiary system serves quite different purposes for different groups in its constituency, and those purposes conflict. Everybody hates and fears it, including its directors, and everybody feels frustrated by it. But only the inmates find it utterly destructive; the people who work there, in whatever rank, are merely angry and resentful that it does not meet their needs more generously and with less difficulty. And those needs have little or nothing to do with the welfare of prisoners, though some officials, and the odd guard, are concerned about that at first.

The MacGuigan Report in no way underestimates the complexity of the circumstances it examines and deplores, and it is not sentimental about what convicts, or other people, are like. But it clearly identifies the hatred, hostility, contempt, and underlying fear of guards for inmates as the major source of the abuses it describes.*

There is, of course, nothing peculiarly Canadian about this factor, which has proved both central and incorrigible in accounting for the lethal conflicts of Attica and virtually every prison in which violence has come to light. It is also true, as the subcommittee notes, that inmates insult and abuse guards when they have the chance. But the roles, after all, are hardly symmetrical, nor are the responsibilities mutual. The guards are supposed to be doing a job—primarily a custodial job, supervising and controlling the movements of other human beings. Instead, they often envision themselves as the prisoners' tormentors. As the subcommittee notes:

> (205) The sentence of imprisonment imposed by the court authorities constitutes the punishment. Those who work in the penitentiary system have no authority, right, or duty, to impose additional

*This conclusion is further verified by the observations of Gerard McNeil and Sharon Vance, who participated in the investigations of the MacGuigan committee and reported their observations independently in *Cruel and Unusual* (Ottawa: Deneau and Greenberg, 1978), chapter 3. McNeil, a parliamentary press gallery reporter better known for his tenacity in carrying to the Supreme Court of Canada a lawsuit seeking to limit the powers of the Nova Scotia Censorship Board, which had barred *Last Tango in Paris* from the province, traveled with the committee, as of course did Vance, a research staff worker for committee member Stuart Leggatt.

> penalties except for proven misconduct during incarceration.
> (206) This may appear to be self-evident, but considering the ten-
> dency among custodial personnel to regard their duty as one of
> punishing prisoners, we think it worth over-emphasizing.

The subcommittee found that inmates were subject to
both physical abuse and vicious taunting disparaging them in
sexual and scatological terms—terms that McNeil and Vance,
who were not inhibited by the niceties of official prose, quote
explicitly. There have been a number of unexplained but violent
deaths of inmates in the past few years, and one slaying of a
young prison official thought to be sympathetic to convicts—
Mary Steinhauser, who was shot by a prison guard at British
Columbia Penitentiary while being held hostage during a revolt
in June 1975. Much of the subsequent inquiry was held *in camera*; and it is probable that the slaying would have continued to
be blamed on the inmates who were holding the hostages—as it
was in initial reports—had not the coroner, whose inquiry *was*
public, insisted that Ms. Steinhauser had been shot to death. Her
captors had only knives.

While most of the abuse, physical or verbal, to which prisoners in Canadian penitentiaries are subject is unimaginative,
there have been exceptions. "(220) At B.C. Penitentiary," the
subcommittee reports, "at least nine inmates in one range
slashed themselves on Christmas Eve 1976 after a guard left two
razor blades in a cell and told them to 'have a Merry Christmas
and a slashing New Year.'" All of this costs the Canadian tax-
payer upwards of $17,000 per man per year, or about the aver-
age Canadian family income—a figure which does not include
the costs of welfare for the prisoner's usually destitute family.
The total number of positions authorized for the Canadian Penitentiary Service at the time the subcommittee reported was
9,429, of which 841 were being held in reserve for programs not
yet fully operational. The total number of inmates, as of April 12,
1977, was 9,374. The ratio of staff to inmates is almost exactly
unity—no luxury hotel or cruise ship could equal that, these
days. The corresponding ratio for U.S. federal penitentiaries is
one staff member for just under three inmates; for the California
system, about the same. This is still, I suspect, a higher ratio
than Hilton hotels provide; but it is only a third as lavish as the

Canadian standard; nor has it been reported to include extra razor blades.

It is usual in reporting abuses such as these to enter a disclaimer noting that prison guards may be good people and that few are sadistic; most are ordinary people doing what is expected of them by their peers and their bosses. The subcommittee confirms this; it also shows that the question of individual psychopathology hardly arises. The basic concepts needed to understand Canadian penitentiaries are social, economic, and of course political rather than psychological; to the extent that they are psychological, the relevant theoretical understanding derives from the conflict theory of Kurt Lewin rather than Freud and the psychoanalysts. Some readers may recall Lewin's classical Robber's Cave experiments, in which boys divided into two quite arbitrary units in summer camp were transformed into hostile groups who behaved toward each other much as guards and convicts do—even the contents of their taunts were similar—though neither group was allowed to dominate the other. The conflict was exacerbated by efforts to get boys from the two groups to mix and get to know each other better; but it was resolved by creating a serious artificial crisis—a break in the camp water supply, for one thing—which could only be remedied by cooperative effort by both groups. Marxian theorists, in turn, would point out that this is just what the prison system must prevent at all costs—that one of the most important functions of the criminal stigma and incarceration is to prevent guards and convicts from discovering that they share a common immiseration as members of the same low social class and might evolve a common political purpose that would enable them to face the solicitor general of the day as a body of 18,000 hostile questioners, perhaps inducing him to respond more specifically than he usually chooses to do.

This is not, however, one of the subcommittee's sixty-five recommendations. Indeed, the subcommittee's findings suggest that, whatever their social origins, the correctional officers of the Canadian penitentiary system are hardly to be regarded any longer as a defenseless proletariat. Guards who would prefer to treat prisoners decently are identified as "con-lovers" and terrorized by their more hostile peers. And whether or not guards enjoy abusing prisoners, many find it profitable to do so. A major motivation for taunting and abusing inmates is to create a crisis in which they can receive extra pay, both for extra risk and for overtime. One guard at Millhaven Penitentiary—probably the most brutal and conflict-ridden in the country at the time of the subcommittee investigation—earned more than $30,000 in this way during the 1976-77 fiscal year. The abused convict may not even be the object of hatred, but of an even more crushing contempt that goads him into providing his tormentors with the opportunity to profit by abusing him further. They can usually do so with impunity, though on just one occasion their actions did prove unprofitable. In October 1977, a former inmate of Millhaven Penitentiary was awarded $15,000 damages in a *civil* suit for injuries inflicted on him by guards during his imprisonment; the guards were also ordered to pay his legal costs. The Crown, however, had consistently refused to act on the *criminal* charges he attempted to bring against his assailants.

One may ask why the prison administration permits this; and, certainly, the MacGuigan committee's central recommendation is that prison directors be given authority which, as modern bureaucrats, they do not now have. Above them, and between the director and the commissioner of penitentiaries—who, under the Office of the Solicitor General, heads the entire system—a network of regional offices was established and interposed in 1961. Directors claim—and the committee concurs—that regional offices interfere with the running of the prison, at least passively by withholding action on essential programs and policies. Recommendation 22 of the MacGuigan Report asserts that "regional offices must not have line management responsibility but should play a consultative, audit, service and support role. They must not interfere with the running of institutions. Divisional instructions must be abolished. . . ." But the correction officers' union, a division of the Public Service Alliance of Canada, is the source of limitations on the director's authority that have far more serious consequences with respect to the maltreatment of prisoners. A prison warden cannot fire any guard without the concurrence of an independent inquiry into allegations of specific misconduct; the union contract provides that. The guard cannot even be transferred, as the warden can. The subcommittee observes:

> (390) There is nothing more mistaken in the entire penitentiary system than the current procedure for disciplining employees. Inability of the administration to discipline staff, even for the most reprehensible breaches of prison regulations, insubordination and gross misdemeanor, indicates a fundamental problem with the rules under the Public Service Staff Relations Act and the governing collective agreements.

It then relates an incident at the "ultra-maximum" correctional Development Centre near Montreal opened in 1968 to house Canada's most "incorrigible" convicts. Its director at the time this incident occurred, Pierre Goulem, "was regarded by some prisoners as a kind of martyr battling for them against hopeless odds," according to McNeil and Vance.*M. Goulem nevertheless yielded to the guards' demands that a prisoner be put into disciplinary solitary confinement—"the hole"—because he had complained about being pulled by the hair. If he were not, the guards threatened to withhold meals from the 109 inmates. From the MacGuigan Report:

> (391) ONE HON. MEMBER: "But what action did you take against the guards?"
>
> MR. GOULEM: "Because of the situation there was nothing I could do. Knowing the hostility of the Alliance, if I had gone against them it would have made things worse the day after."

Recommendations 26 and 27 of the *Report of the Sub-Committee on the Penitentiary System in Canada* read:

> The Penitentiary Service under the board must be an independent agency of government not subject to the *Public Service Employment Act* or the *Public Service Staff Relations Act*. It should resemble the R.C.M. Police in its discipline and professionalism. Employees should be subject to discharge for misconduct or incompetence.
>
> Employees of the Penitentiary Service who perform supervisory or confidential functions should not be entitled to belong to unions. Matters clearly under the prerogative of management such as security,

*Ibid., p. 58.

programming and inmate welfare must not become the subject of collective bargaining. Compulsory arbitration must be the only means of dispute settlement.

It is difficult to disagree with the thrust of these recommendations; the solicitor general responded by establishing "a working group consisting of senior officials from CPS, the Ministry of the Solicitor General, the Privy Council Office, Treasury Board, and the Public Service Commission" to consider them. If the group is doing so, the results of its deliberations have not so far been reflected in changes in policy. But even if they should be, and should lead to some improvement in the treatment of convicts in Canadian prisons, they still reveal the fundamental limits imposed on the committee by its own attitudes toward authority.

Within a year of the time the MacGuigan Report was released, the McDonald royal commission—often with apparent reluctance—had revealed many reasons why the RCMP can scarcely be taken as a model of organizational discipline from which to design a new and improved Penitentiary Service. The fact that the MacGuigan committee could, at this point in time, have thought that it might be, suggests the degree to which it is in fact hung up on authority—on the conviction that more and tighter, though also more rational, control is the most promising approach to difficulties arising from excessive oppression in the first place. By its own account, the committee knows that such an approach cannot get to the heart of the problem. The second* of its sixty-five recommendations states flatly that "the criminal justice system should be carefully re-examined with a view to enlarging the alternatives to incarceration." This recommendation follows a closely reasoned nine-paragraph analysis, which begins:

(189) Society has spent millions of dollars over the years to create and maintain the proven failure of prisons. Incarceration has failed in its two essential purpuses—correcting the offender and providing permanent protection to society. The recidivist rate of up to 80 percent is the evidence of both.

---

* Actually the first, since the initial recommendation merely declares: "A crisis exists in the Canadian Penitentiary System. It can be met only by the immediate implementation of large-scale reforms. It is imperative that the Solicitor-General act immediately on this Report as a matter of the most urgency."

In a sense, then, the *Report of the Sub-Committee on the Penitentiary System in Canada* is a massive exercise in bad faith, which its candor and forthrightness of detail serve partly to mask. There is no way that imprisonment can contribute either to the rehabilitation of prisoners or, in any significant degree, to the security in person and property of those members of society who, for one reason or another, remain outside prison walls. The subcommittee noted as much itself. That it nevertheless proceeded to set forth a series of recommendations intended to improve conditions in Canadian prisons is not really astonishing; this is what we have come to mean by being realistic. Prisons are here to stay—the Government of Canada, while the MacGuigan Report awaits consideration, is building twenty-four new ones—and it seems reasonable to offer recommendations intended to make incarceration less inhumane, however marginally, even while expressing no confidence in its social value.

It *seems* reasonable; but it probably is not. In fact, the temperate and conservative tone of the report has made it no more influential than a less courteous approach might have been. The first recommendation, demanding immediate action on the report, has gone unheeded; the concluding recommendation, that

> the Standing Committee on Justice and Legal Affairs should have a permanent reference during the rest of the 30th Parliament and for the 31st Parliament to enable it to review the implementation of this Report in the context of the criminal justice system,

was immediately rejected by the solicitor general. Moreover, the committee's fundamental recommendation—"Directors must have the power and authority to manage their institutions," unchallenged save by the authority of the commissioner of penitentiaries—seems especially unlikely to lead to serious change if considered in the light of observations in Gordon Hawkins' authoritative monograph, *The Prison.** The relevant passages oc-

---

*(Chicago: University of Chicago Press, 1976). Hawkins, a former assistant principal of the United Kingdom Prison Staff College and director of the Long-Term Young Prisoners' Centre at Wakefield Prison, was associate professor of criminology at the University of Sydney, Australia, at the time *The Prison* was published. The "book was written during the tenure of a research fellowship at the Center for Studies in Criminal Justice of the University of Chicago Law School" (p. xi). Professor Hawkins writes from as extensive an experience of prison life as any scholar not also a convicted felon could hope to do.

cur in a section of the book in which Hawkins is considering the traditional reluctance of the courts to intervene to sustain the civil rights of prisoners. Following a concise discussion of the sanctions inflicted on the militant black prisoner Martin Sostre in New York State in response to litigation he had *successfully* mounted in quest of religious liberties for Black Muslims, Hawkins observes:

> The Sostre case was not an isolated instance. Goldfarb and Singer offer numerous similar examples of what happens when prison administrators have absolute, unreviewed discretion (1973). And it is that which is the crucial issue. Hirshkop and Millemann make the point: "Prisoners often have their privileges revoked, are denied right of access to counsel, sit in solitary or maximum security or lose accrued 'good time' on the basis of a single unreviewed report of a guard. When the courts defer to administrative discretion, it is this guard to whom they delegate the final word on reasonable prison practices. *This is the central evil in prison*. It is not homosexuality, nor inadequate salaries, nor the cruelty and physical brutality of some of the guards. The central evil is the unreviewed administrative discretion granted to the poorly trained personnel who deal directly with prisoners. The existence of this evil necessarily leads to denial of communication, denial of rights to counsel and denial of access to the courts. Prison becomes a closed society in which the cruelest inhumanities exist unexposed." (1969, pp. 811-12; [Hawkins'] italics)*

Two pages further on, Hawkins continues:

> Rights to freedom of speech and assembly, to enjoy privacy, to vote, and to communicate freely, which have been held elsewhere to be protected by the [U.S.] Constitution, have not in the prison setting been recognized as among the "fundamental, humane, and necessary rights" whose breach violates the Constitution. Within narrowly described areas judicial rulings have resulted in increased freedom for inmates, but for the most part the discretion of correction and prison authorities has not been seriously limited or subjected to regulation.
>
> Indeed, whatever may be the situation regarding the particular rights mentioned above, it seems that the really crucial question in this context is that of regulating the discretion of prison administrators.

*Ibid., p. 139. The references cited by Hawkins are to Ronald L. Goldfarb and Linda R. Singer, *After Conviction* (New York: Simon and Schuster, 1973); and Phillip J. Hirshkop and Michael A. Milleman, "The Unconstitutionality of Prison Life," *Virginia Law Review*, 1969, *55*, 795-839.

Hirshkop and Milleman are right in their assertion that "unreviewed administrative discretion" is "the central evil in prison." This is because the pursuit, recognition, enforcement and enjoyment of all other rights are ultimately dependent upon the prison authorities' exercises of that broad discretion which they claim is necessary for the preservation of order and discipline and which, despite some inroads, they still to a very large degree possess unimpaired.*

It is clear that Hawkins and the Subcommittee on the Penitentiary System in Canada are in general agreement as to what the evil aspects of prison life in fact *are*; and they begin to agree on the underlying cause—that is, abuse of authority by poorly trained and often hostile guards. But they clearly disagree completely as to how that abuse may best be checked. Hawkins turns to the constitutional guarantees, noting regretfully that the courts, too, tend to sustain authority rather than human rights when their petitioner is a convict, but despairing in any case of seeking justice within the confines of the penitentiary itself. The subcommittee's approach, however, is primarily elitist and, in this regard, very Canadian. The guards are to be controlled, not by enforcement of guarantees of basic human rights within the prison by judicial process—for even free Canadians possess, in fact, no such formal guarantees—but by granting more authority to directors of prisons, who, it is assumed, will choose to run their institutions firmly but fairly.

The MacGuigan Report demands to be accepted as an act of faith in the eventual triumph of the Canadian sense of fair play and devotion to the dignity of man, an act of faith which sees fit to ignore a wealth of empirical evidence that these, though doubtless of normal strength, are not trustworthy bases for confidence that penal reform is a cause which will find enough political support to get it moving, in Canada or anywhere else. Prison reform is a poor political risk in any country, for reasons that Hawkins states very clearly:

> Powerful constraints on change operate . . . which not only impede progress in penology but render prediction in this sphere more than usually problematic. One of these constraints is the prisoners' lack of any political leverage. Another is the operation of the principle of less eligibility, to which I have already referred. In this context the

*Ibid., p. 141.

principle requires that the condition of the prisoner should be inferior, or at least not superior, to that of the lowest classes of the non-criminal population in a state of liberty. There is no doubt that this principle, which underlies much of the common thinking about the treatment of criminals, has always constituted a formidable barrier to penal reform. And it is surely illusory to anticipate that in the field there is any likelihood that we will move rapidly forward. Progressive politicians and correctional administrators who assume that penal reform is widely accepted as A Good Thing which reasonable people everywhere will automatically endorse are no more realistic than those whose distaste for the twentieth century induces them to keep their gaze fixed yearningly backwards.*

The *Report of the Sub-Committee on the Penitentiary System in Canada* ignores these political realities in arriving at what would otherwise be a set of reasonable and modest proposals. Why was the subcommittee willing to go as far as it did? By its own account, because a crisis existed in the Canadian penitentiary system, which had recently been plagued by repeated incidents of violence and brutality. Hence the emphasis on discipline; but it would have been easy, and more acceptable to public opinion in Canada, to have used this term in its most repressive sense. That the subcommittee did not is, I think, genuine evidence of one of the best things about Canadian political life. It is still small enough in scale that the members of Parliament who composed the committee, though supported by a sixteen-person staff, did their own fieldwork and saw for themselves what was happening in Canada's penitentiaries, especially its maximum-security institutions. They were personally affected by what they saw, while their endearingly archaic commitment to discipline undoubtedly made it easier for them to speak the truth—clearly, though with much reserve. A commitment to discipline is ideologically important to public life in Canada. It is a fundamental item of false consciousness and serves to assure the public that gravity of demeanor on the part of public servants means that Something Will Be Done. With virtually no avenues open to subsequent freedom of inquiry in Canada, there is little risk to the authorities in allowing it to be supposed that some redress of grievances is under consideration.

*Ibid., pp. 41-42.

But why, in fact, is it so likely that little or nothing will be done to improve conditions in penitentiaries—both generally and in Canada, in particular? Neither of Hawkins' constraints is so totally self-evident but that it bears reexamination. In a sense it is obvious that prisoners lack political leverage—otherwise they would pry themselves out of prison—but this fact raises more questions about the nature of the criminal justice system than it answers. And the "principle of less eligibility," though heuristically useful, is simply one aspect of what has come to be called "the politics of resentment," which is the context in which the whole question of crime and punishment is embedded. The penitentiary system, which seethes with resentment and exists to provide an outlet for even greater resentments than it contains, gives an excellent point of departure for a somewhat more systematic consideration of this issue and its slightly but crucially different manifestations in Canadian and American life.

It seems clear that the "principle of less eligibility" provides the unstated basis for the assumption by Canadian prison guards that it is *their* job to punish convicts, rather than the function of the courts. No convict, it is assumed, has a right to make himself more contented than, or have self-esteem equal to, a prison guard; and prison guards in Canada, in view of their high rate of turnover, low socioeconomic status, and hostility and petulance as revealed in the subcommittee report, are not very contented and seldom have much self-esteem. I would suspect that the "relative benignity" of U.S. federal prisons, where officers are said to "treat you like a man" by prisoners comparing conditions to those in state penitentiaries,* is closely related to the observation recorded in the MacGuigan Report that "(257) in the United States we found that penitentiary work was an attractive career for persons of exceptional ability because, among other reasons, merit could be recognized and rewarded through promotional opportunities that were not blocked by an accumulation of senior officers waiting out their time for retirement until age 65 or so." While authoritarianism is likely to be relatively high among any group of persons who choose to earn their living as prison guards, and tends in any case to lead people to vent their

*Ibid., p. 88.

frustrations on those subject to their will, the "principle of less eligibility" tends to make it also their moral duty to see that no prisoner is less miserable than themselves. Canadian prison guards apparently are often miserable.

In this connection, an editorial which appeared in the *New York Times* for Monday, June 6, 1977, is worth rather careful attention. The editorial concerns a beating that occurred in the state prison at Attica, New York, on July 11, 1976, five years after the riots which made the place infamous, took forty-three lives—mostly of inmates—and led to the indictment of sixty-two inmates and no guards, as well as to the promise of substantial reforms:

Attica: Who's in Charge?

An argument now raging among the New York State Department of Correctional Services, the Attica corrections officers' union and the State Commission on Corrections may strike some as a lot of "Who-struck-John?". But who struck Albert McQueen in Attica prison on July 11, 1976, and why, and under what circumstances—and why don't we know eleven months after the event—are questions of great consequence to the way the prison system functions in this state.

Some of the facts are clear. Albert McQueen, an Attica inmate and an important spiritual leader there, was injured during a search of his cell at 9:15 on a Sunday night. So were at least two of the guards who participated in the search. Shortly thereafter, 50 inmates staged a riot, which led to an eight-day prisoner strike—all this raising the specter of the bloody 1971 uprising at the prison. There have been three inquiries: by a Wyoming county grand jury; by the Department of Correctional Services, which runs the state prisons, and by the Commission on Corrections, a watchdog group.

Their findings do not jibe. The grand jury—sitting in a county where jurors have been notably sympathetic to their neighbors, the corrections officers—found no evidence of criminal offense by the guards. The Department of Correctional Services found no cause to discipline any officers, but decided that the procedures for searching cells required clarification and tightening. The Commission on Corrections concluded that a beating of Mr. McQueen by five guards had precipitated the riot and strike and noted with displeasure that of 22 subpoenaed officers only 9 came to its hearing and only one of them agreed to testify—to the effect that he had not seen the McQueen incident.

Confronted by this confusion, Correctional Services Commissioner

Ward has called an open hearing to require the testimony of the reluctant guards. The guards, in turn, are charging that the Commission on Corrections always sides with the prisoners. They threaten to
strike if the hearing is held.

Once again, therefore, the difficulty of prying information out of a
necessarily closed prison community threatens to overwhelm public
authority. Once again group conflict threatens to turn a small incident into a tragedy. Whatever the claims of other groups, the role of
the Department of Correctional Services is crucial; its authority over
the guards should be automatic, and never subject to negotiation. Re-
views of violent incidents ought to be routine, as they are in the New
York City Police Department. All parties would know that they
could be heard, and that they had to participate. The essential facts
would be established long before memories dimmed and battle lines
formed.

One need not agree with the *Times'* reference to the beating of Mr. McQueen as a "small incident" or accept quite so
readily the "difficulty of prying information out of a necessarily closed prison community" in order to see that the problems
encountered by the New York State Commission on Corrections are very similar to those reported by the parliamentary
subcommittee. They include the threat of a strike if a vigorous
investigation is pursued, and the probability of collusion among
guards to make that investigation fruitless.

"Whatever the claims of other groups, the role of the Department of Correctional Services is crucial; its authority over
the guards should be automatic, and never subject to negotiation." The language might have been that of the MacGuigan
committee rather than of the *New York Times*. But though
they reach identical central recommendations with respect to
authority, a critical difference in tone remains. The *Times*, even
in a short editorial, sounds harassed by the complexity of the
whole situation and makes no suggestions as to how the authority of the Department of Correctional Services might be established and maintained. The MacGuigan committee, however, is
quite clear and cool. It knows, and it says, how the problem
should be attacked. The solution for the failure of authority is
more authority: model the Penitentiary Service after the highly
disciplined RCMP.

It is not my intent to deride the recommendation itself,

which might result in some improvement. The RCMP are, in fact, usually brought in to replace striking Canadian prison guards as a stopgap measure and things do usually become calmer; they don't treat the prisoners as badly, though this may be because the latter are strangers to them and the status-rooted patterns of hostility do not have time to develop. I know very little about penal reform—indeed, I do not believe it to be possible—and would not choose to write on it. My purpose in this discussion is, rather, to show how Canadian institutions respond to what Canadian society has defined as a serious social problem: with massive doses of authority even when their own analysis reveals that abuse of authority lies at the heart of the problem.

The administration of authority can be useful; in limited emergencies it may be crucial to survival, to getting things going again until homeostasis reestablishes itself. But authority is a powerful depressant and extremely addictive. Like other tranquilizers, authority is prescribed to solve problems that have been mistakenly diagnosed, and whose real roots it cannot touch and serves, in fact, to obscure. The criminal sanction appears to provide an almost ideal-typical case. I have already noted that the MacGuigan Report argues in support of its very first substantive recommendation that incarceration be phased out and alternatives to it be found, on the grounds that the 80 percent recidivism rate shows that it serves neither to alter criminal propensities nor protect society from criminal acts. The argument that "you have to do something about crime; you can't just let them get by with it" cannot be used to justify imprisonment at all. You don't have to do something that demonstrably doesn't work.

Indeed, the argument that "you have to do something about crime; you can't just let them get by with it" is false and misleading in itself, even if imprisonment were not the customary, and ineffective, sanction. Why do you have to? Because violence to individuals and willful misappropriation of property are something decent Canadians cannot tolerate? They do tolerate it, in the form of highway accidents that could have been prevented by enforcement of existing legislation; industrial pollution that violates not only existing statutes but specific cleanup orders previously accepted by private corporations and the government itself. In both these cases, the number of victims, including fatalities, can be predicted quite accurately; and all the potential Hillside stranglers and 44-calibre killers who might be at large in Canada could not hope, collectively, to win even a bronze medal in competition with INCO and its fellow industrial giants.

The difficulty isn't that Canadians couldn't bear the risks involved in closing their prisons or even abandoning the criminal code itself. It is, rather, that they couldn't bear the thought. The political and economic consequences would be enormous. Political, because imprisonment does effectively stigmatize those subjected to it, effectively barring many persons whose hostility, impulsiveness, or reasoned antagonism to the existing social order would make them its very dangerous adversaries in a fair fight. Imprisonment—not just conviction or the admission of guilt—keeps them from ever attaining the status from which they could operate effectively. In this sense, the recidivism rate can be viewed as a *positive* social indicator; it suggests how hard it is for a man with the skills and attitudes required of a competent if occasionally unsuccessful bankrobber to establish himself in a legitimate position in society.

Economically, of course, law enforcement is one of Canada's most lucrative industries. The Penitentiary Service costs around $200 million a year to run; but that is small change compared with the costs of providing it with raw material. As McNeil and Vance wryly observe:

> The number of police in Canada had grown to 50,000 in 1975 from 32,000 in 1965. It was a decade in which alarmed citizens were ready to pay anything to have the drug trade suppressed. And pay they did.
>
> As the number of police grew, so did the pay cheques. By 1975, a first class constable drew triple the salary for the rank ten years earlier. And his $18,000 a year did not include overtime, which was unknown in 1965. The cost of the RCMP alone was $627.5 million in the 1977-78 fiscal year. It had been $75.9 million in 1965-66. The force by now had 19,000 members, double the 1965 total.*

Neither the dollar figures nor these on numbers of personnel reflect, of course, the prevalence in Canada of paid informers

*McNeil and Vance, op. cit., p. 164.

and clandestine operations. Truly, crime contributes to the economy: it creates jobs, it even adds to the gross national product as this is customarily calculated. And all this rests on the backs of about 25,000 poor—mostly very poor—souls in jail. Most of them are less than 30 years old and have never finished school; a disproportionate number are native people. In what other way could these few—these gallant if not happy few—impoverished in body and mind and often even in spirit, contribute so much to their country?

4

Structural Obstacles to Liberty under the Canadian System of Government

The Government of Canada, as has been noted, operates under the doctrine of parliamentary supremacy. Parliament is the ultimate source of legal authority in the land. There are certain *structural* limits to parliamentary authority; but there are no *substantive* limits.

Canada has a Constitution, of course; much of it, like the British Constitution, unwritten and derived from the British Common Law, which is replaced in Quebec by a written Civil Code of Procedure. But its formal basis is a written—though not a Canadian—document. As has been noted, this is the British North America Act passed by the Parliament at Westminster on March 29, 1867, which incorporated the existing, separate colonies of Canada (Ontario and Quebec), New Brunswick, and Nova Scotia into the single Dominion of Canada and made provision for the subsequent inclusion of other Crown colonies— most recently, Newfoundland in 1949. In 1949, the British Parliament also expanded the rights of the Parliament of Canada to amend the Constitution except with respect to language rights, the rights reserved to provincial jurisdiction, and the five-year maximum duration of Parliament itself—though even this may be suspended, with its own consent, in times of "apprehended insurrection." No constitutional limits are set to the apprehensiveness of the Canadian government.

Canadians are currently very much concerned about their Constitution and its limitations. Both a Special Senate Committee and a Special Joint Committee of the Senate and the House of Commons on the Constitution of Canada were established during the 1978 session of the Thirtieth Parliament. The October 1978 Conference of First Ministers (that is, the prime minister and the premier of each province) was devoted largely to constitutional issues prompted by Quebec's threat of separation— Premier René Lévesque was present and seemed unusually cool, calm, and collected—and to Canada's poor economic conditions, which intensified the customary conflict between the federal and provincial governments over regional disparities and rights to natural resources. One television commentator, paraphrasing the American journalist S. L. Clemens, noted on this occasion that in Canada the Constitution had replaced the weather as the topic everybody talks about and nobody does anything about. Canada's native peoples have grown so concerned that in the summer of 1979, they sent a delegation to London to persuade the Queen of Canada to insist that they be included as participants in current discussions of constitutional changes, as they have not previously been. Acting on the advice of her Canadian ministers, Queen Elizabeth declined to see them.

But when Canadians become concerned about their Constitution, they are usually worried about issues that are very different from those that Americans would regard as constitutional. The government frequently brings up the matter of "repatriation" of the Constitution, which means removing even the last vestiges of British control over the processes of its amendment. But neither the provincial premiers nor the Canadian people take this issue very seriously; nor should they. Westminster is not the problem; the British domination Quebecers fear comes from Ontario and points west, not from England. Indeed, the last previous effort to repatriate the Constitution a few years ago was frustrated only because the Quebec legislature, which is already called—perhaps prophetically, perhaps not—L'Assemblée Nationale, refused to ratify it. When M. Trudeau pled the urgency of repatriating the Constitution, Canadians usually responded by accusing him of trying to distract them from more practical issues like inflation and unemployment. If so, the stratagem did not succeed.

Canadians and, most importantly, the Supreme Court of Canada, view the Constitution primarily as an instrument whose function is to establish the limits of jurisdiction of different branches of government and especially of provincial and federal agencies and legislation with respect to one another. The Constitution of the United States, of course, also performs this function through the Tenth Amendment, which reserves to the states or to the people all powers not specifically awarded to the federal government by the Constitution. But the heart of the British North America Act is to be found in Section 91, which lists twenty-nine different specific areas of jurisdiction that are exclusively federal, and Section 92, which lists sixteen that are exclusively provincial. Some of these are so detailed as to seem rather petty, like Item 9 on the federal list, which reads "Beacons, Buoys, Lighthouses, and Sable Island," though the recurrent rumor that natural gas is about to be discovered on Sable Island makes even this a proper subject for jurisdictional dispute between the Government of Canada and that of Nova Scotia, off whose shore Sable Island lies.

But to most Americans, the Tenth Amendment is hardly the heart of the Constitution or even of the Bill of Rights, which it concludes. Americans, when they think of their Constitution, rely on it primarily as an instrument that protects them from intrusion by *any* government—local, state, or federal—in certain crucial areas of their lives. The first five words of the First Amendment go directly to the heart of the matter: "Congress shall make no law. . ." The Bill of Rights then goes on to specify what it is that Congress shall make no law about; and these excluded areas define what Americans regard as their fundamental human rights.

To those who are concerned with understanding the crucial differences between the Canadian and American systems, however, those first five words are more important even than what follows. In practice, Canadians enjoy most of the same rights Americans do, though in lesser degree; the Canadian Bill of Rights, though not regarded as a part of the Constitution of Canada, refers to substantially the same areas of human action and interaction. But those rights are not *guaranteed* in Canada. Under the system of parliamentary supremacy, they cannot be; for not only is Parliament permitted to intrude into any area it chooses, there exists at present no legal instrumentality by which it might be forbidden to do so—except, that is, by a finding of the Supreme Court that under the BNA Act, or occasionally some other statute, the provinces and not the federal government got there first.

Under the doctrine of parliamentary supremacy there can be no separation of powers among the judicial, legislative, and executive branches—the two doctrines are antithetical. The problem is not that Canada lacks an independent judiciary. The Canadian judiciary is independent to the point of paranoia. During the Trudeau government, one cabinet minister was cited for contempt of court for referring to a judicial decision that cost Canadian consumers millions of dollars in higher prices for sugar as "insane," though that was surely the most charitable interpretation possible, while another was threatened with this action and forced to apologize because he had telephoned a judge to discuss a case dealing with a matter then under judicial consideration but lying within his area of administrative responsibility. Canadian judges at whatever level are appointed, never elected, so as to preserve them from any popular pressure. The idea that certain judicial posts are filled by election in the United States is one of the features of American government that Canadians tend to find shocking. The problem is that the courts in Canada are without authority to limit the regulatory intent of Parliament on any substantive—as distinct from jurisdictional —grounds.

For this reason, the question of *entrenchment* of the Bill of Rights—that is, its incorporation into the Constitution so that it becomes paramount law, instead of, as at present, one statute among all other statutes—presents peculiar difficulties. The first two sections of the Canadian Bill of Rights—which contain all its substance (the remaining section requires the minister of justice to examine any legislation subsequently proposed to Parliament and call to the attention of the House of Commons "provisions inconsistent with" the Bill of Rights) read:

1. It is hereby recognized and declared that in Canada there have existed and shall continue to exist without discrimination by reason of race, national origin, colour, religion or sex, the following human rights and fundamental freedoms, namely,

   a) the right of the individual to life, liberty, and security of the person and enjoyment of property, and the right not to be deprived thereof except by due process of law;

b) the right of the individual to equality before the law and the protection of the law;

c) freedom of religion;

d) freedom of speech;

e) freedom of assembly and association; and

f) freedom of the press.

2. Every law of Canada shall, unless it is expressly declared by an Act of the Parliament that it shall operate not withstanding the *Canadian Bill of Rights*, be so construed and applied as not to abrogate, abridge or infringe or to authorize the abrogation, abridgment or infringement of any of the rights and freedoms herein recognized and declared, and in particular, no law of Canada shall be construed or applied so as to

a) authorize or effect the arbitrary detention, imprisonment, or exile of a person;

b) impose or authorize the imposition of cruel and unusual treatment or punishment;

c) deprive a person who has been arrested or detained

(i) of the right to be informed promptly of the reason for his arrest and detention

(ii) of the right to retain and instruct counsel

(iii) of the remedy by way of *habeas corpus* for the determination of the validity of his detention and for his release if the detention is not lawful;

d) authorize a court, tribunal, commission, board or other authority to compel a person to give evidence if he is denied counsel, protection against self-incrimination or other constitutional safeguards;

e) deprive a person of the right to a fair hearing in accordance with the principles of fundamental justice for the determination of his rights and obligations;

f) deprive a person charged with a criminal offence of the right to be presumed innocent until proved guilty according to law in a fair and impartial hearing by an independent tribunal, or of the right to reasonable bail without just cause; or

g) deprive a person of the right to the assistance of an interpreter in any proceedings in which he is involved or in which he is a party or a witness, before a court, commission, board or other tribunal, if he does not understand or speak the language in which such proceedings are conducted.

An Act for the Recognition and Protection of Human Rights and Fundamental Freedoms, of which the Canadian Bill of Rights is the operative section if it may be said to have one, received royal assent and became law on August 10, 1960. In addition to the Canadian Bill of Rights, the act includes an orotund preamble with the usual references to the supremacy of God—not Parliament—and the dignity of men, and a second part consisting of three brief paragraphs intended to establish the way in which the Canadian Bill of Rights should be construed. The first of these states that "nothing in Part I [that is, in the Canadian Bill of Rights itself] shall be construed to abrogate or abridge any human right or fundamental freedom not enumerated therein that may have existed in Canada at the commencement of this Act." The second paragraph merely defines "law of Canada" for the purposes of the act as including not only statutes but any regulation for which Parliament bears responsibility. The third, however, declares:

> The provisions of Part I shall be construed as extending only to matters coming within the legislative authority of the Parliament of Canada.

A noble, if belated, document, this Act for the Recognition and Protection of Human Rights and Fundamental Freedoms. How well, then, does it recognize and protect those rights and freedoms?

Very badly indeed; in fact, it must be recognized that Section 2 of the act disclaims, at the outset, any intention to provide the sort of absolute protection of rights and freedoms that the Bill of Rights affords under the Constitution of the United States. "Every law of Canada shall, unless it is expressly declared by an Act of Parliament that it shall operate notwithstanding the *Canadian Bill of Rights* . . ." But the precise intent of the U.S. Bill of Rights is to affirm that "Congress shall make no law" which contravenes the provisions of the Bill of Rights. Where the Canadian Bill of Rights reserves to Parliament the final decision as to whether a protected right shall be abrogated in a particular instance, the American is designed from the outset to place these rights beyond the reach of Congress.

As Walter S. Tarnopolsky, author of the definitive and

classic work on the Canadian Bill of Rights,* noted in his statement before the Special Senate Committee on the Constitution (August 10, 1978),† the authors of the Canadian Bill of Rights debated, at the time of its consideration by Parliament in 1960, whether a request should be made to the British Parliament that *it* also introduce the Canadian Bill of Rights as an amendment to the British North America Act so as to make it indisputably a part of the Constitution. They decided that this would accomplish nothing, since the BNA Act as amended in 1949 already empowers the Parliament of Canada to amend any part of the act that pertains only to federal jurisdiction. In order to expedite passage of the Canadian Bill of Rights, Prime Minister John Diefenbaker had accepted the final clause, already quoted, which restricts the application of the Canadian Bill of Rights to matters within the jurisdiction of Parliament, thereby avoiding the necessity of seeking ratification by the ten provinces, which he felt could not have been obtained. Diefenbaker was undoubtedly correct in this belief; even today, eighteen years later, several of the premiers at the October 1978 Conference of First Ministers spoke out against the establishment of the Bill of Rights as constitutional law—which would make it binding on the provinces—precisely on the grounds that it would limit the authority of Parliament. That, among other things, is precisely what an effective Bill of Rights must do. But by agreeing to limit the Canadian Bill of Rights to matters within the jurisdiction of Parliament, its authors also guaranteed that Parliament would have the power to amend it. Since they also gave Parliament the power to pass valid legislation that "shall operate notwithstanding the *Canadian Bill of Rights*," it is hard to see why it would have to. But it could, anyway; the point is that, in Canada, Paraliament itself has substantial power to amend the Constitution. In the United States, Congress has none.

It is difficult, therefore, to see how an effective Bill of Rights could ever be entrenched in Canada. Tarnopolsky, in-

---

**The Canadian Bill of Rights*, 2nd ed. (Toronto: McClelland and Stewart, 1975).

†*Proceedings of the Special Senate Committee on the Constitution*, Issue No. 4 (Hull, Quebec, Printing and Publishing, Supply and Services Canada, 1978), p. 8.

deed, continued his presentation to the Special Senate Committee by arguing that it need not be, because, "whether or not one has entrenchment, the likelihood of a bill of rights being amended so as to weaken it is extremely rare"* —a statement both curiously phrased and curiously optimistic. A far stronger argument against entrenchment of the Bill of Rights was placed before the Special Senate Committee on September 7, 1978, by James C. McRuer, former chief justice of the High Court of Justice of Ontario, president of the Canadian Bar Association in 1946-47, and one of Canada's most distinguished jurists. Justice McRuer tartly observed:

> It has been the history of entrenched bills of rights that the courts have distorted the language of such a bill to give it entirely different meanings. . . . Those who favour entrenchment seem to have an idea that they would get better decisions from the courts if the rights were entrenched. Time and again it has been said that the way the Supreme Court of Canada has dealt with cases arising under the Bill of Rights has been unsatisfactory. It would be that much worse if they were entrenched, because if the Bill of Rights is not entrenched and not satisfactory, amend it and get it right. But you then have the guidance of what the court has held it does not apply to. If it is in the public interest to correct the court's decision, that can be done by Parliament or the legislature.†

This argument, of course, begs the question, central to the function of a Bill of Rights, as to how the individual may be protected *from* the legislature as well as by it. The pertinence of Justice McRuer's remarks, however, is evidenced by the celerity with which the Supreme Court of Canada, in numerous decisions —especially by Mr. Justice Roland A. Martland and Mr. Justice Roland Ritchey—evolved what Tarnopolsky has called the "frozen concepts theory of interpretation." Section 1 of the Canadian Bill of Rights, it will be recalled, declares

> that in Canada there have existed and shall continue to exist without discrimination . . . the following human rights and fundamental freedoms, namely . . .

and then proceeds to enumerate them. This is the sort of re-

*Ibid., p. 12.
†Ibid., Issue No. 6, pp. 28, 30.

sounding claim that might better, perhaps, have been placed in the Preamble. But it is, in fact, a part of the operative section of the act; and the Supreme Court lost no time in interpreting it in a way that would seem quite the contrary of the act's stated purpose—"the Recognition and Protection of Human Rights and Fundamental Freedoms." The Court held that the statement just quoted meant that the Bill of Rights could *not* be considered to have granted the people of Canada any *new* rights. The rights to which it referred were the rights they had always enjoyed and always would enjoy. Consequently, in a case in which it was argued that the Lord's Day Act contravened freedom of religion by requiring all shopkeepers to observe the Christian Sabbath, the Court held that the Lord's Day Act could not be held to conflict with the Bill of Rights, because the right to conduct a business on Sunday was clearly not a right that had always existed in Canada. The same reasoning was unfortunately also applied in the matter of capital punishment; it couldn't be a cruel and unusual punishment contravening the Bill of Rights, because the right not to be hanged was not a right that had always existed in Canada. Note that in both these instances—and the "frozen concepts" doctrine was applied in a variety of other cases as well (or as ill)—the Canadian judicial custom of avoiding confrontation with the *substantive* issue in the case was maintained. The Supreme Court of Canada could have held, as that of the United States did and as the chief justice of Canada, Mr. Bora Laskin, did in a concurring opinion, that the death penalty was not, in fact, cruel and unusual per se, though it might well be so in a particular case. But the majority opinion relied on "frozen concepts." The fact that in this instance Parliament did respond, for the present at least, by abolishing capital punishment instead of relying on judicial construction, provides some support for Mr. Justice McRuer's position.

Still, McRuer's warning that entrenchment would make the Bill of Rights even more vulnerable to judicial castration by impairing the power of Parliament to restore those functions it intended to provide after a restrictive judicial interpretation had removed them, derives its pertinence from the fact that Canadian courts, during the scant two decades since the bill was passed, have so often chosen to interpret the bill restrictively. Canadian society is ideologically committed to "peace, order, and good government" as higher values than life, liberty, and the pursuit of happiness, or at least as the essential preconditions to the maintenance of these endowments. In their relationship to liberty, peace, order, and good government are indeed valuable as *pre*conditions; without them, life and liberty are difficult to maintain and happiness, fugitive at best, tends to elude pursuit all the more easily. But peace and order do not of themselves insure that liberty will be protected; through history they have been—and are—far more frequently purchased at the cost of liberty. It all depends, after all, on what one means by "good government." If Canadians regard the protection of liberty as a major test of whether government is good or not—and the very fact that an Act for the Recognition and Protection of Human Rights and Fundamental Freedoms was finally passed indicates that the notion is, after all, accorded a certain importance —their government is constructed throughout to sacrifice liberty to the demands of order and, indeed, to the convenience of the government in power, when serious conflicts arise.

Some of the mechanisms for tilting the balance in favor of authority have already been discussed—such as the Federal Court Act, which denies the courts the power to subpoena any evidence whose revelation the solicitor general or any other minister of the Crown designates as injurious, and which, moreover, declares the decision of the minister to lie beyond the power of any court to review. It is easy to react with such shock to the content of the Federal Court Act that one neglects the significance of the basic principle it invokes, which is ubiquitous in Canadian administrative practice. In Canada, as in the United States and other industrialized societies, the lives and business of residents are regulated by countless bureaucratic agencies whose rulings have the force of law. In Canada, however, there is usually no right of public access either to their deliberations or to their records; and their rulings are usually protected by the same kind of immunity as that provided by the Federal Court Act. Ultimately, under the doctrine of parliamentary supremacy, the decision whether to reveal any information or justify any decision rests with the minister of the department that has jurisdiction—often only after the fact—over the bureau involved. There is no appeal from his refusal to respond, nor any legal remedy available should response prove inadequate. If the issue becomes public—and in any area deemed related to national security even this may be forbidden—the cabinet minister is subject to questioning by Opposition colleagues in the House of Commons, as, of course, is the prime minister himself. But parliamentary debate is hedged about with formalities and restrictions. Members of Parliament seem, on the average, usually better educated and more articulate than congressmen; their questions are generally sharp and clearly phrased; the answers as often effectively evasive.

For, as noted toward the beginning of this work, and despite my emphasis on parliamentary supremacy, Parliament is hardly supreme. The cabinet is. There are now some thirty cabinet portfolios in Canada; posts are created, abolished, shuffled, or combined as the prime minister of the day may require. A minister may be appointed to serve without portfolio if the prime minister wants him in the cabinet and no post is vacant; or he may give a minister he relies on more than one portfolio. Otto Lang, member for Saskatoon-Humboldt in Saskatchewan and a staunch Liberal wheelhorse who at different times held portfolios as varied as justice, transport, and manpower and immigration, held three at once for a short period before he lost his seat and the Liberals were swept from office in the 1979 general election.

The cabinet holds the real political power in Canada. Cabinet minutes are Canada's topmost secret, denied even to the McDonald commission *in camera*; the principle of cabinet solidarity precludes any member of the cabinet from differing publicly with a position once taken. It would be fair, if excessively polite, to say that cabinet decisions are reached by consensus rather than ballot. These decisions, when proclaimed by the governor-general as orders-in-council, have the force of law.

Under the Canadian system, the idea of contravention of an order-in-council by Parliament as a whole is literally meaningless—that is, it corresponds to no imaginable parliamentary process. Nor can orders-in-council normally be subjected to judicial challenge; the order may even include a provision making it unlawful to reveal its existence, as was the case with the device by which the Government of Canada sought to conceal its participation in an international agreement to raise the price of uranium by 49 percent—successfully, until an American congressional committee investigating price fixing in the uranium industry disclosed it. In this case, the order was apparently unlawful under both American antitrust legislation and the Canadian Combines Act. It prevailed, nevertheless.

Perhaps the most revealing, and certainly the most extreme, example of the scope of orders-in-council is to be obtained from a reading of the War Measures Act. It is this act, it will be recalled, which though passed as a measure designed to empower the government to deal with acts of insurrection, espionage, or the collapse of civil authority in wartime, has remained on the books and was invoked to suspend civil liberties in Canada during the so-called October crisis of 1970. The act is no anachronistic curiosity which Parliament has simply neglected to repeal. In fact, it was amended after passage of the Canadian Bill of Rights with a clause reading simply and clearly:

> Any act or thing done or authorized or any order or regulation made under the authority of this Act, shall be deemed not to be an abrogation, abridgement, or infringement of any right or freedom recognized by the *Canadian Bill of Rights*.

So much for the human rights and fundamental freedoms that have existed and shall continue to exist in Canada, the "frozen concepts" doctrine notwithstanding.

The War Measures Act is itself, of course, an act of Parliament; but it is invoked by order-in-council. It contains a rather complex provision by which the two houses of Parliament acting concurrently may revoke it, "but without prejudice to the previous operation . . . or anything duly done or suffered thereunder or any offence committed or any penalty or forfeiture or punishment incurred." There would therefore seem to be serious grounds for fear that the governor-in-council might invoke the War Measures Act in undue haste or panic, without sufficient evidence that a threat to the nation sufficient to justify the suspension of all civil liberty existed. Happily, Parliament anticipated this danger, and abolished it in the very first paragraph of the act following its title:

The issue of a proclamation by Her Majesty, or under the authority of the Governor in Council shall be conclusive evidence that war, invasion, or insurrection real or apprehended, exists and has existed for any period of time therein stated and of its continuance, until by the issue of a further proclamation it is declared that the war, invasion or insurrection no longer exists.

When the act is in force:

for greater certainty but not so as to restrict the generality of the foregoing terms, it is hereby declared that the powers of the Governor in Council extend to all matters within the classes of subjects hereinafter enumerated, namely,

a) censorship and the control and suppression of publications, writings, maps, plans, photographs, communications and means of communication;

b) arrest, detention, exclusion and deportation;

c) control of the harbours, ports and territorial waters of Canada and the movement of vessels;

d) transportation by land, air, or water and the control of the transport of persons and things;

e) trading, exportation, importation, production and manufacture;

f) appropriation, control, forfeiture and disposition of property and of the use thereof.

Until October 1970, the War Measures Act had never been invoked except when Canada was, in fact, at war; and the Canadian people could hardly have been expected to be concerned about its continued presence on the books. It may have been thought of as the kind of reserve power any state must retain, such as that provided in Article 1, Section 9, of the Constitution of the United States: "The privilege of the writ of *habeas corpus* shall not be suspended, unless when in cases of rebellion or invasion the public safety may require it." There is, of course, a striking contrast between this laconic statement, whose major thrust is to *forbid* the suspension of the civil liberty except under conditions of what the Supreme Court of the United States has come to define as "a clear and present danger," and the seemingly lascivious detail with which the War Measures Act enumerates the areas in which the governor-in-council may exercise autocratic power, after carefully specifying that this enu-

meration is no restriction, in case the act happened to leave anything out. Still, no war, no war measures, the Canadian people
were entitled to think until October 1970. But nearly 90 percent
of the population approved Prime Minister Trudeau's invocation
of the act, in a crisis marked by two kidnappings and the mur-
der of one of the kidnap victims—a high-ranking provincial
civil servant and Liberal politician—after the act had been invoked. The hundreds of arrests and incommunicado detentions
resulted, finally, in only two prosecutions. For more than two
years after the act was allowed to lapse again, the political climate remained sufficiently hysterical that witnesses before the
Keable commission continually referred to it in justifying the
kinds of illegal and quasi-terroristic actions—break-ins, barn
burning, and the like—of which the RCMP were accused. At
this point, surely, faced with the evidence that what Canadian
authorities required in times of temptation was restraint upon
their fantasy rather than license to act it out, the Canadian elec-
torate ought to have had second thoughts about the War Measures Act in particular and civil liberties in Canada in general.

    And, indeed, this is happening—though on how wide a
scale it is difficult to say. Certainly, civil liberty is a salient moral and political issue in Canada today, as it never has been in the
past. But it is far from a popular cause. In this respect, the structural provisions of the War Measures Act are perhaps more fundamentally disturbing than its admittedly Draconian substance.
What state of mind, politically, begins such an act by metaphys-
ically enthroning the authority of the governor-in-council, declaring him to be the sole witness of political reality? What the
governor-in-council—that is, the cabinet—apprehends "shall
be conclusive evidence" that what is apprehended, is so. This is
an invitation, literally, to self-delusion; no paranoid could ask
for more. But there is method in this madness; it exactly parallels the denouement of *The Mikado*: "When Your Majesty says
let a thing be done, that thing is as good as done—practically it
is done—and if it is done, why not say so?" It will be recalled
that the Mikado accepted this logic with a grateful smile, declaring: "I see. Nothing could possibly be more satisfactory!"

    The defense of liberty by litigation in Canada can seldom
proceed by an assertion of principle. It consists, customarily,

of a broken-field run around the province in order to take refuge behind the federal government or vice-versa, according to the circumstances. The process and, alas, the results, from a civil libertarian viewpoint, are often rather bizarre. No example can be clearer than that presented by a recent case in which Gerard MacNeil, co-author of the book *Cruel and Unusual* cited in the previous chapter, attempted to combat motion picture censorship in his home province, Nova Scotia.

MacNeil, at that time a member of the editorial staff of the Dartmouth, Nova Scotia, *Free Press*, filed suit against the Censorship Board of the province contesting its right to forbid the showing of *Last Tango in Paris*. Canadians seem seldom aware of the activities of such boards because they seldom bar standard commercial films outright, but content themselves with demanding that offensive scenes be cut and assigning a "Restricted" rating that makes it unlawful for persons younger than the province's minimum age—usually 18—to attend the film even with their parents. But the Nova Scotia board had become bolder, barring in recent years films like *A Clockwork Orange* and *Drive, He Said*, as well as *Last Tango in Paris*.

When MacNeil first filed suit against the Censorship Board, the province of Nova Scotia contested his right even to file the suit, on the grounds that as a private citizen he had no standing in the matter. It argued that, as a citizen, he had no basis on which to claim a right to be allowed to see a film; only an exhibitor with a putative commercial interest in the matter had such a right. MacNeil therefore had to sue the province and win even to gain the right to take the Censorship Board to court. He did; but it cost him more than a year, and most of his savings. Nevertheless, having gained the preliminary victory, he set about the far more costly and time-consuming task of trying to win on the merits of his case, with the full knowledge that *this* case would have to be carried all the way to the Supreme Court of Canada and won there, as the province would surely appeal any victory he might win in the lower courts.

There would appear, on the face of it, to be two possible logical avenues of approach to a question of obscenity. One, of course, is to argue that the work in question is not, in fact, obscene; that it has redeeming social value, or does not, on balance, despite the presence of some offensive material, exceed the limits set by prevailing community standards or whatever the basis of existing anti-obscenity legislation may be. This is the usual approach of the defense when faced with a charge of obscenity; but it would not have served MacNeil's purpose at all. No exhibitor was being prosecuted for showing *Last Tango*; none in Nova Scotia had had the temerity to try. MacNeil was a plaintiff, not a defendant. Furthermore, the approach is inherently too limited to achieve the end MacNeil sought, which was not just to gain access to a particular film by convincing the courts that the Nova Scotia Censorship Board misjudged it, but to question and if possible reduce the board's power to determine what films he might see.

The second approach, then, is to challenge the right of a government to censor a work at all, on what in the United States would be First Amendment grounds. This has been attempted in many cases in the United States, of course, though the Supreme Court has never, in fact, upheld the absolute right to freedom of expression that the simple language of the First Amendment would seem to support (in the view of Mr. Justice William O. Douglas, probably the strictest constructionist of the First Amendment the Court has ever known). The attempt, in any case, has the very considerable virtue of honesty and relevance—refreshing in a legal argument. It raises the right issue, whether the argument prevails or not, while arguing that a particular film or book is not obscene in order to get it before the public not only begs the question but sometimes appears to violate what any reasonable man would judge to have been the author's manifest and perhaps glorious intent.

But in Canada there is no First Amendment, and no legal basis on which such an argument could be advanced. Obscene publication is an offense against the criminal code. Since, however, Section 91, Article 27, of the British North America Act reserves criminal process to federal jurisdiction, the very fact that obscenity is a criminal offense would appear to have provided a strong prima facie case, under Canadian law, against the authority of a provincial agency to define or restrain obscene publication.

Because, as has been indicated, the rulings of the Supreme

Court of Canada with respect to the validity of statutes are almost always made on jurisdictional grounds, MacNeil was emboldened to proceed upon his costly and time-consuming undertaking. And he won his case in the court of first resort; Nova Scotians enjoyed a year or so free of motion picture censorship while the decision awaited a hearing, on appeal by the province to the Supreme Court of Canada. The waiting period was a rather tense one for civil libertarians. The legal validity of the decision against the exercise of censorship by a province seemed evident; yet it was difficult to imagine that the Supreme Court of Canada would break with tradition and with the mood of the country to support absolute freedom of expression. So improbable did it seem that, far from becoming a deluge of previously forbidden fruit during the interregnum, the pattern of available motion pictures scarcely changed. *Last Tango* and *A Clockwork Orange* were finally screened, it is true, but motion picture exhibitors, on the whole, continued to show restraint rather than provocative films. This was also a time in which the cause of the Canadian filmmaker was being strongly promoted as necessary to the defense of Canadian culture and national unity; and it is sometimes difficult to imagine, let alone produce, a really juicy obscene film with 85 percent Canadian content. *Peut-être, nous n'avons pas de quoi.*

In due course, to be sure, the Supreme Court of Canada reversed the decision of the lower court and restored the power of provincial censorship boards. It did so by reaffirming, in effect, the basis for the argument that the province of Nova Scotia had advanced unsuccessfully in its effort to deny MacNeil standing at the outset of his litigation. Section 92 of the BNA Act assigns "Property and Civil Rights in the Province"—"civil rights" in this sense refers to matters like contract rights or marriage rights, enforceable in civil litigation, not to civil liberties—and this was held to cover the rights that motion picture exhibitors might or might not have. Freedom of expression, finally, was not the issue; and under Canadian law there is no way MacNeil could have made it the issue, though he bankrupted himself in the attempt.

Clearly, the structure of any government reflects the interaction of a variety of complex factors: historical, political, economic, psychological. There is no sense in which the government of a country, whether democratic or despotic, can be said to express or reveal the present will of its citizens undistorted by historical or economic constraints. But, conversely, it is equally clear that no government can remain stable which grossly and systematically violates the will, or at least the patterned expectations, of its citizens. The government need not give them much that they want or need; it may have neither the resources nor the techniques necessary to do so. But what it does do must somehow fall within the range of what has come to seem appropriate. The government must be perceived by most of the people most of the time as doing what a government is supposed to do, for better or for worse. This, after all, is what the legislators who drafted the Canadian Bill of Rights meant to convey by referring to the rights enumerated therein as rights that "have existed and continue to exist" in Canada.

By the same token, it must be granted that no tradition was broken, or expectation outraged, when the Supreme Court of Canada eviscerated the Bill of Rights by a trick of schoolboy logic more worthy of an Eton College debating society than of a high tribunal. Canadians are often annoyed when their officials adopt the style of British public school boys—television critics have almost stamped out the House of Commons tradition of drumming on one's desk as a way of applauding—but they are not astonished. Canadian elites have been gleefully outwitting the peasantry for the sake of order and good government since the Family Compact ruled Ontario in the 1820s and, indeed, far earlier. When Cornwallis surrendered to Washington at Yorktown, the British military band, it is reported, played an air called "The World Turned Upside Down." It must have seemed so, indeed; but among the loyal colonies to the north, nobody shook it hard enough for anything to fall out.

It would be presumptuous, therefore, to think of Canadian society as having been deprived of liberty by an archaic governmental structure and a weak Constitution. Of themselves, and in the absence of an established tradition of individual autonomy, formal constitutional guarantees may avail nothing; they may even be a lethal trap, as the highly libertarian Constitution of the Soviet Union has been for those naive enough to claim what it purports to guarantee. Canadians do not lack entrenched civil liberties because their form of government makes it difficult to provide them; they accept a governmental structure under which liberty cannot be guaranteed because they are highly ambivalent about personal freedom and because they genuinely believe that government is designed to be an instrument for advancing the general welfare, and is not, in principle, anything to fear. Canadians are often bitterly critical of particular governments, as Shakespeare was of particular kings. But Shakespeare believed in royalty; it was precisely this belief which informed him as to what a good king should be and laid the moral basis for his trenchant criticism of bad ones. Few Canadians seemed to share the perception that has become an American commonplace: that government is essentially a political apparatus which interested parties struggle to gain control of in order to better gain their own ends; this struggle *is* the political process.

Canadians are sometimes scandalized by the actions of public officials; but since those actions are not seen from a critical perspective, such scandals do not clear the air—they make it more oppressive. Late in the autumn of 1978, John L. Farris, the chief justice of the province of British Columbia, resigned from the bench, forfeiting his position and his pension because the Vancouver vice squad had found his name in a prostitute's notebook. Mr. Justice Farris made no statement either defending or explaining his position. A fortnight or so after the revelation, the provincial bar association announced that an investigation had revealed no evidence that the justice had acted unlawfully; and since he had resolved the question of impropriety by resignation, the matter was now closed.

By these actions, the justice and his critics collaborated to reassert a conventional social norm about the need for judges to behave impeccably, thereby protecting Canadian society from an opportunity to raise some really serious questions about its own operations. Must justices sacrifice themselves at the mere imputation of possible sexual misconduct? One might suppose that they have a prior obligation to defend the right of any accused, including themselves, to be presumed innocent until proven guilty. The judiciary in Canada seldom questions either the value or the probity of the conduct of law-enforcement officials; might the justice have gained a broader understanding of the importance of civil liberties on finding his career so seriously threatened by the publication of an unsubstantiated police report? Apparently not, since he did not raise this question. If the justice had, in fact, been a client of the young woman whose documents the vice squad had seized what, exactly, made this a matter so serious as to justify his resignation? Merely conventional outrage at an offense against public standards of morality? Or was there a stronger feeling that a justice of the Supreme Court of British Columbia must have more respect for women than to use them in this offensive way? Or a still deeper feeling that a man who bears the responsibility of passing judgments that determine the fate of other human beings must not feel himself so loveless and alone—or even so hopelessly old-fashioned? If these considerations affected the course of events in any way, that fact was not reported in the national media. In the face of impending scandal, the important task was to reassert the sanctity and purity of the Bench, not to consider the human predicament of this judge; and no one could have acquiesced in this position more fully than Mr. Justice Farris himself. To have defended himself, or even to have sat tight, would have been to let Canadian civilization down.

Yet perhaps there is another kind of heroism and dedication to public service to be considered: that of Congressman Adam Clayton Powell, suing to defend his right to retain his seat in the House of Representatives despite efforts to remove him for criminal misconduct—and winning, on the grounds that the voters' choice must be honored, however dishonorable the candidate might subsequently be. Or Mayor Curley of Boston, years ago, refusing on the same grounds to resign his post and conducting the affairs of the city of Boston from his cell in the Federal House of Correction in Danbury, Connecticut, returning to his desk after serving his sentence as if nothing had happened.

Canadians like to believe that they hold their public servants to a higher moral standard than do Americans. A Watergate, they say, could never happen here, though by this they often mean that a series of firm and timely orders-in-council would have terminated public disclosure. For this reason alone, they are right; a Watergate could not happen here. But there are deeper reasons, which have nothing to do with the question of whether Canadian officials behave better than American. The more important point is that, when abuses do occur, the right questions are seldom raised publicly in Canada—not, at least, until a royal commission has pondered the matter for several years before issuing an incisive report: incisive, but not too loud. The structure of government, as we have indicated, makes it almost impossible to raise them publicly or to demand meaningful answers. But, surely, this is true only because more powerful Canadians don't like such questions to be raised—even if they don't particularly want the answers concealed, it's still bad form —and less powerful Canadians find confrontation with their adversaries embarrassing and frightening rather than invigorating.

But, paradoxically, the Canadian commitment to good government in principle acts, I believe, as a major barrier to the establishment of the sense of national identity that Canadians now so anxiously and continually seek. One cannot easily identify with a nation conceived as so queenly and pristine. The difficulties are almost Freudian. The Government of Canada comes to resemble the good, Victorian mother to whom it is impossible to attribute the sort of conduct that is necessary even to account for one's own birth. Conversely, there is a strong tendency to feel that whatever is really vital about oneself and realistic about one's response to others and to social situations is wrong, punishable, and, at worst, ego—alien. Realism, especially political realism, comes to seem un-Canadian. But one cannot really feel oneself securely a part of a family whose highest virtue is chastity; a strong identity must be based on more affirmative action.

5

An Economy
of Deference

One of Canada's most persistent and serious problems is foreign economic domination. Though pervasive in its effects, the process can hardly be called insidious. Foreign domination, economic and cultural, is a fact of Canadian life—a fact of which Canadians are keenly aware and of which they frequently complain. It is an issue in federal election campaigns, perennially exploited by the nominally socialist New Democratic Party, which has very little difficulty finding a recent and convincing reason for again accusing the government of the day of selling still another chunk of Canada to the Americans. Comparable deals with German, Japanese, Chinese, or Arab principals are less likely to be condemned and may, indeed, be welcomed by Canadians because they both stimulate the economy and reduce its dependency on solely American investment.

The Government of Canada has frequently established commissions of inquiry to consider the effects of foreign ownership on the Canadian economy. In 1955, Walter L. Gordon, the distinguished financier who would later become minister of finance in the Liberal government of Lester B. Pearson, chaired a Royal Commission on Canada's Economic Prospects which, two years later, produced a "decidedly nationalistic" report that, according to an American scholar, "rank[s] in scope, penetration, and even eloquence among the very best ever produced by Canada's many Royal Commissions."* In 1963, as minister, Gordon con-

*John S. Dickey, *Canada and the American Presence* (New York: New York University Press, 1975), p. 106.

fronted James S. Rockefeller, who was seeking to take over, on behalf of the First National City Bank of New York, a Dutch-owned bank already established in Canada. This would have been legal under the Canadian legislation existing at the time, though the takeover was sharply limited, and further such efforts forestalled, by new legislation passed in 1967, shortly after Mitchell Sharp had replaced Gordon as minister of finance. (Sharp himself was later to be strongly criticized by advocates of social democracy and human rights for Canada's policy in *support* of Canadian investment in Chile during his tenure as secretary of state for foreign affairs from 1968 to 1974.) Dickey gives this account of the deficiencies in Rockefeller's awareness of Canadian attitudes toward American investment:

> In January 1967, when the then head of Citibank, James S. Rockefeller and a number of his principal associates appeared before a committee of the House of Commons to oppose the proposed restrictive legislation, the committee indicated its incredulity that a bank of Citibank's international position had undertaken the acquisition of a Canadian chartered bank without being aware that such a transaction would not be welcomed in Canada, and, indeed, would be in direct conflict with the previously publicized position of the Minister of Finance.
>
> The response of Mr. Rockefeller suggests how long ago 1963 was: as to his knowledge of Walter Gordon prior to discussing the matter with him in July 1963, he knew only that he "was an accountant" and was regarded as "a very nice gentleman"; asked whether he had not known of Gordon's strong feelings about foreign ownership, he replied:
>
> "No, I certainly did not. . . . Mr. Gordon's attitude was a shock to me; it was such a surprise. Neither was I familiar with the famous book at that time, you know. . . . We did not get this feeling of nationalism, or whatever you want to call it. We consider ourselves friendly neighbors." *

With friends like these, who needs commissions of inquiry? Canada does; and has had several devoted to the question of foreign economic domination. In 1968, Melville H. Watkins chaired a government Task Force on Foreign Ownership and the Structure of Canadian Industry; what he learned in the course of that

*Ibid., p. 109.

activity led to this conclusion, expressed in the New Democratic Party's "Waffle Manifesto" in 1969: "The major threat to Canadian survival today is American control of the Canadian economy. The major issue of our times is not national unity, but national survival, and the fundamental threat is external, not internal." In 1970, another committee, the Standing Committee on External Affairs and National Defence of the House of Commons, identified as "its principal effort . . . a basic examination of relations with the United States." The committee was especially concerned about cultural domination and particularly the special provisions of the Income Tax Act, which allowed advertisers to deduct the costs of advertisements placed in *Time* and *Readers' Digest*, but not in other general circulation foreign magazines—a privilege of which *Time* was soon to be stripped. Both magazines published special Canadian—but not very Canadian—editions. But in 1971, the cabinet received, but did not release, a memorandum entitled "Domestic Control of the National Economic Environment: The Problems of Foreign Ownership and Control," usually known as the Gray Report after its principal author, the Honorable Herb Gray, then minister of national revenue. This is the report that, as I noted earlier, *Canadian Forum* courageously and unlawfully published in abridged form more than six months after the cabinet had received it. In 1972, the government finally published the report under the title, *Foreign Direct Investment in Canada.*

The Gray Report is not the product of a royal commission —it is simply a memorandum to the cabinet—but it surely merits all the praise Dickey lavished on the earlier report of the Gordon commission. It is not anti-American in tone; but it is totally uncompromising in its delineation of the economic plight in which Canada finds itself as a consequence of its largely foreign-dominated economy. Details have changed in the years that have passed since its publication, but it seems unlikely that the basic problems will ever be more clearly stated or their consequences more tellingly described. They are familiar; they include the brain drain and stunted technical development characteristic of branch-plant economies whose research and development and policy planning are carried out elsewhere; the continued imposition on Canada of the unprofitable role of hewer of wood and drawer of water, supplying raw materials for complex and profitable processing into finished goods in the United States or elsewhere; and the shifting to Canada of the least profitable aspects of production generally for the purpose of keeping taxes down. Only one condition that Gray found an intolerable affront to Canadian sovereignty has vastly improved since the report was made public. In 1971, nominally Canadian branch-plant firms often found themselves prevented from fulfilling legitimate and lucrative contracts with foreign—usually communist—countries by provisions of American legislation that threatened their executives with prosecution for trading with the enemy. This unseemly exercise of extraterritoriality seems to have been stopped, partly by strict Canadian legislation acting as a counterthreat, partly through diplomatic pressure by Canada on the United States, and most of all, perhaps, by the curious change in the American political climate manifested by the wave of Sinophilia that has swept away not only American objections to trade with China but the competitive advantage Canada gained from its early recognition of Mao's regime.

No reasonable person, surely, would seek to minimize the effects of foreign ownership on the Canadian economy and, through the economy, on Canadian culture. The facts are too well established and have been too frequently reconfirmed to admit doubt. There is, of course, more room for divergence of opinion as to how these facts should be interpreted. Canada's dependence on dominant American economic interests leave her in a position analogous to that of a wife in a marriage of convenience in a male-dominated society. The convenience is mutual, but unequal. When a conflict of interest arises, the husband's convenience usually prevails; he may not even notice that the wife resents this and the imputed slight to her own identity, and is neither as happy nor as faithful as he supposes her to be. Nevertheless, from the point of view of the conventional social system they both share, the wife does derive certain advantages: protection from physical and economic threat—along with greater liability to such threats, since she is now involved in her husband's quarrels—and a larger share of the world's resources than she could earn by her own, unsupported efforts

——though not as large a share as she might have earned had she not been thrust into a subordinate role in the first place.

Some women, of course, bring to marriage a sense of resignation——preferring it to spinsterhood, the world being what it is, but bitterly regretting the freedom and autonomy they have renounced. So, no doubt, do some nations come to terms with their unchosen status as satellites of more powerful neighbors, especially if——like Poland, for example——they have an ancient tradition of struggling, usually unsuccessfully, for political and economic freedom. Canada, however, has no such tradition. On the contrary, the crucial turning points in its development as a nation have been the decision of the colonies to continue to adhere to England at the time the American colonies revolted; and later, in 1867, the formation of the Dominion of Canada by an act of the British Parliament. Canada had nationhood, if not independence, thrust upon it. The fact that one of the two major original colonies included in confederation had been conquered from France by British military force more than a century earlier and had retained its French language and culture under guarantees from the British Crown has continued to make the rest of Canada cling the more firmly to its English tradition, perpetually uneasy about "the French fact"——which is nevertheless fundamental to the nation's Constitution.

Canadian complaints about foreign economic and cultural domination, though very soundly based, are nevertheless in some ways culturally dissonant; they don't really fit the Canadian tradition. Canadians have enjoyed colonial status for centuries. The Québecois have not been enjoying it as much lately, but even they have a far less libertarian tradition than the French, for Quebec was won from France thirty years before the French revolution and never came to share its ideology. Even New Zealand, which comprises the two most British isles in the world, retains its Anglitude more through isolation than through defensiveness, though the British sense of cultural superiority doubtless contributes to the isolation. But the colonies that formed Canada in 1867 had by that time retained for nearly a century, as a matter of policy, the colonial status the American colonies had rejected in 1776.

Canada's current and chronic concern about its national

identity has its roots—or lack of roots—in the protracted assumption throughout the nation that its myths and heroes were British rather than Canadian. Even the Québecois, as they become increasingly restive about domination by English Canada, conceive of it as precisely that, not as a struggle between two regions of the country with conflicting values and economic interests, like the War Between the American States. Even the schools —ordinarily the strongest bastion of nationalism—until very recently in Canada indoctrinated pupils with a British rather than a specifically Canadian loyalty. Robert M. Stamp, in his report "Empire Day in the Schools of Ontario,* gives a detailed and startling account, based on the records of the time, of this annual celebration of imperial authority by which Canadian children were taught to honor their British rather than their indigenous cultural heritage.

Empire Day began to lose its grip on the Canadian imagination in the wave of disillusionment that followed the First World War, though "the 1931 parade was the largest ever as some 13,750 cadets and 1800 girls marched along the traditional route up University Avenue to Queen's Park" † in Toronto. Despite the stimulus to patriotism Anglophone Canada derived from World War II, even the term "Empire Day" disappeared during the 1950s, to be replaced by "Commonwealth and Citizenship Day" and, ultimately, just "Citizenship Day," which occasioned little pageantry; this is now saved for Dominion Day, July 1, when schools are not in session. Victoria Day, a Monday in Mid-May, also closes the country down completely, as it has since 1845. Meanwhile, as Canadians have sought increasingly to make themselves *maîtres cheux eux*, American hegemony has replaced and in some ways surpassed that of Britain.

A familiar and rueful Canadian joke holds that, while Canada had hoped to achieve a synthesis of British governance, French culture, and American know-how, it has been left, instead, with the residue of British know-how, French governance, and American culture. What nobody suggests is that Canada has

---

*Included in Alf Chaiton and Neil McDonald (eds.), *Canadian Schools and Canadian Identity* (Toronto: Gage Publishing, Limited, 1977), pp. 100-15.

†Ibid., p. 110.

ever assumed that it might be Canadian through and through, though it has voiced that aspiration with mounting anxiety in recent years. Despite the real problems created by foreign economic domination, the cultural anxiety seems misplaced. There ain't, as the saying goes, any place anything like this place within miles of this place; so this must be the place. What confuses Canadians is the fact that a propensity to yield to—indeed, to seek—economic domination by others is itself one of the most distinctive and deeply rooted historically of Canadian characteristics.

How, then, does one assess the effects of foreign economic aggression on the development of Canadian society? Canadian society has, indeed, often been rudely penetrated by organs of foreign intervention, though usually with the consent of Canadian interests and government of the day. Even the most militant of Canadian nationalists concede the complicity of their government and ruling elites; indeed, it is precisely that which angers them most and makes them feel most betrayed. That anger may be justified; it is indeed probable—though hardly self-evident —that the resulting exploitation has stunted and distorted Canada's economic development. The question is, compared to what? Compared to what Canadians might have done with those same resources—if only Canadians were different?

As an adult member of the family of nations, Canada is to be presumed capable of informed consent: a circumstance that is damaging to the charge of rape by American or other intruders. Even today, in light of the analysis made in the Gray Report and continued criticism from radical Canadian intellectuals with a lot of compelling evidence on their side, the victim remains undecided about really trying to evict the intruder and slam the door on him, despite the immediate costs. The failure to do this, or at least seriously to attempt it, cannot be compensated by uttering sporadic cries of indignation. What is most interesting about the Canadian case is not that Canada has been economically exploited by foreign investment on unfavorable terms. Canada, itself, has drained off considerable wealth from Caribbean and South American states and, more recently, from Indonesia, if Canadian foreign investment is to be judged by the same criteria as American; while banks in both countries have provided and continue to provide essential support for the South African regime, which consumes the majority of its own people. All this is deplorable and, if the means can be found to forestall it, intolerable; but it has also, unhappily, become commonplace.

Canadian openness to economic exploitation is not commonplace, however; it is as remarkable as the most venomously anti-American Canadian critics maintain. And it is in certain respects paradoxical. Rueful references to the hugeness and restlessness of the American giant do not explain it. Neither Japan nor Germany, though ruined, conquered, and occupied by the military forces of that giant, have in fact been ravaged by it; the economic relationship that has developed between the United States and these two former adversaries is complicated, and it is by no means clear at this point who is doing what to whom. Compared to Canada, these countries are poor in resources and have expanded economically to the limit of their native labor supply and beyond. I am not suggesting that they are to be emulated; Canada, I am sure, is a pleasanter place to live than either, for reasons that are linked to its relative underdevelopment. But they are not, and do not consider themselves, America's economic pawns; at worst, they are antagonistic cooperators—partners in a grossly profitable and excessively private enterprise.

But Canada does seem to have inordinate difficulty in resisting the economic domination it finds so threatening, despite its potential wealth. Canadian banks are notoriously reluctant to finance new Canadian enterprises; they prefer to lend to larger, already well-established—and often foreign-dominated—firms. Both the federal and provincial governments have programs through which loans may be made and tax exemptions granted to promote economic expansion, especially in economically depressed areas of the country; but these are often funneled through chartered banks as government-guaranteed loans and are, in any case, administered by local elites with a tendency to think small—small enough, certainly, to avoid anything that might establish serious competition for the interests in which they are already involved. The result is the channeling of inadequate funds into the support of enterprises that are so marginal, so bizarre, or already so badly crippled that the risks involved are exceptionally high: like the obsolete Sydney Steel Corporation in Nova Scotia, which the government cannot afford to abandon in a part of the country where the economy is in ruinous condition, but which it will not spend enough money on to modernize and make truly competitive; or the infamous Bricklin automobile plant in New Brunswick, which a panicky provincial government forced into bankruptcy just as it began producing some novel and interesting automobiles—and this, if it had succeeded, would again have been an American enterprise and a rather flashy one. So would the ill-fated oil refinery in the appropriately named Newfoundland outport, Come-by-Chance, which the American petroleum financier John Shaheen abandoned after inducing the federal and provincial governments to spend millions developing the port facilities for supertankers and rewarding the officials who had supported him with a well-catered cruise to and from the site on the *Queen Elizabeth II*, chartered for the occasion. In poverty-ridden Atlantic Canada, especially, investors—private or public (though usually public funds are involved)—handle their money like peasants trapped by their greed as well as their naiveté into making stupid investments and then pulling out of those that might have been successful in the long run if they had had the courage and the resources to stick with them.

In an article entitled "Letter from Ottawa: The Sorry State of Canadian Nationalism" (*Harper's Magazine*, June 1975), the distinguished Canadian novelist Mordecai Richler, musing on the curious reluctance of Canadians to seize economic opportunity with the vigor needed to develop and operate their own economy, observed:

> Our problem, unique in the Western world, perhaps, was not an indigenous buccaneering capitalist class, indifferent to those they exploited, yet intrepid and imaginative nation-builders. Our problem was the Scots; the most inept and timorous capitalists in the West. Not builders, but vendors, or, at best, circumspect investors in insurance and trust companies.

> If the pre-World War I American boy, at the age of sixteen, was dreaming of how to conquer and market the rest of the globe, his Canadian equivalent, at the same age, was already seeking a position with an unrivaled pension scheme.

And so, Canadian branch plants proliferate, there's an imbalance, corrections are called for. But mindless, impassioned objection to all things American is a fool's solution. It's no answer.

In fact, the Canadian disinclination to take risks, as evinced through obstacles to foreign trade, has contributed and continues to contribute, paradoxically, to the proliferation of branch plants. Because of high and continuously manipulated tariffs and import quotas and embargoes, foreign entrepreneurs who want to compete on the Canadian market have usually been obliged to acquire Canadian branch plants and produce their goods in Canada rather than export them to Canada. Economically, this is not very efficient. Canada is not Malaysia or the Philippines; wages and production costs tend to be higher in Canada than in the United States. The branch plant presumably represents less of a net drain on the Canadian economy than the importation of foreign goods; but it still leaves Canadian consumers paying higher prices than they would either if free trade were permitted or if Canadian enterprise were more efficient. As it is, small, inefficient Canadian enterprises are often triply subsidized by Canadian taxpayers: by government grants or tax concessions needed to keep them going and support the local economy; by higher prices—eggs and poultry, to note a persistent and egregious example, usually cost about half again as much here as in adjacent parts of the United States; and, in recent years, by the generally higher costs people pay for living in a country whose currency has been depressed by chronic economic inefficiency. All this has certain positive consequences, of course; it creates jobs, as Canadians are fond of saying, though perhaps fewer than a healthier economy would provide; and it permits people to go on living—"living, and partly living," as T. S. Eliot put it in a very similar context—in the community in which they have established roots and ties, long after there is anything of value to the rest of the world to occupy them there.

Intellectual stagnation soon develops in a community that has lost its economic function. Economic protectionism in Canada, though not explicitly designed as a form of censorship, does also establish barriers to communication from abroad; and some of them are gross. A few seasons ago, the Canadian press did raise quite an outcry—without apparently eliciting much response—when CBC television abandoned plans to broadcast a production of the Stratford Shakespeare festival because ACTRA, the Canadian radio and television performers' union, had insisted that foreigners like Maggie Smith and Brian Bedford be replaced, for TV purposes, by their Canadian understudies. The fact that the targets of Canadian protectionism were, in this case, British rather than American doubtless contributed to the volume of protest but did not, in the event, make it any more effective.

The regulations concerning advertising in foreign media also hamper communication in some annoying, though not very serious ways. I have already referred to the hassle in Parliament a few years ago over the special status that made advertisements by Canadian business in the Canadian editions of *Time* and *Readers' Digest* tax deductible. The result was the termination of *Time*'s special status. *Time* responded by discontinuing its special edition, which used to include a comically inadequate section on Canadian news as a kind of preface. *Readers' Digest*, however, which is published in Quebec and provides a large proportion of the jobs available in its community, continued to be recognized as Canadian. What seems offensive in this matter is certainly not the withdrawal of *Time*'s special status—*Time* continues, in any case, to publish an unmarked Canadian edition, as it does regional editions in the United States, but without a special Canadian news section and with a much reduced volume of advertising—but the legislation to which that status was an exception. For this also makes it illegal to import for sale in Canada any foreign journal that includes advertising directed specifically at a Canadian market, even when no tax deduction is involved. The *New Yorker*, for example, which is widely available on Canadian newsstands—so far, at least—and which frequently carries multipage advertisements promoting tourism by Americans in Canada, cannot carry information telling Canadian readers where in Canada they might buy any of the things advertised there. If it did, the issue including such an advertisement would be subject to confiscation at the border and, if the offense were repeated, the magazine could be compelled to suspend distribution in Canada. Similar restrictions apply to television advertising, and have aroused rancour. Canadian businesses cannot deduct the cost of advertising on American TV stations, and this, after all, is Canada's business. But the Canadian Radio-Telecommunications Commission has also been blacking out commercials on American programs broadcast by Canadian cable stations, even though these programs are obtained at fees sharply reduced by the subsidy which American advertising provides.

Foreigners of course have no presumptive right, moral or legal, to advertise in Canada, and Canadians face more serious deprivations in life than being denied American advertising and local TV commercials. Network commercials, with Canadian coloring injected, find their way to the Canadian living room via CBC or the private Canadian television system, CTV, anyway. What is compromised by these restrictions is not freedom of information but freedom of opportunity: the freedom of the Canadian businessman to seek the best value for his advertising dollar and the freedom of the Canadian customer to locate what he wants to buy most cheaply and conveniently, even though he may have to pay duty on it when he brings it home. The result is to add a few more bricks to the protectionist wall, diminishing by yet another small increment the self-confidence needed to function effectively in the larger world and the competence needed to function at home. It is easy to accept protectionism as a familiar and legitimate expression of nationalism; when a people become anxious about their national identity, they are usually culturally and economically protectionist as well. And Canadian nationalists like the Committee for an Independent Canada, which developed from the "Waffle Manifesto," are insistently protectionist—culturally as well as economically.

Yet, in light of Canada's historical tradition, the effort to protect Canada from external influences and domination cannot, in fact, be attributed to nationalism, as it now usually is. Egerton Ryerson, as chief superintendent of education for Canada West—that is, Ontario—fought bitterly to rid his bailiwick of American textbooks twenty years before confederation, with a view to replacing them with British texts. The fight against American influence was as bitter then as it is now, although the issue of specifically *Canadian* content did not arise seriously for another century.

What is at issue here is fundamental to anyone seeking to understand the peculiar quality of Canadian nationalism up to the present day, especially its more exaggerated fears of American domination, legitimate as those fears often are. It is so natural and, indeed, so admirable for any people to insist on defending their peculiar culture and special view of the world against foreign domination, exploitation and, ultimately, as in the case of the native peoples of North America, obliteration, that it seems equally natural to respond with indignation to their cries of alarm and to fight in their defense. But in Canada's case the situation is complicated by a history of earlier acquiescence. Canada is a unique nation with a distinctive culture of its own, just as Canadian nationalists insist. The problem is that one of its most significant and distinctive features is its willing acceptance and even celebration of its own colonial status. That has now all but lapsed, though Canadians, unlike Americans, have never formally rejected it. But what can a people who take pride in having fought and died in the wars of their imperial masters, in a police force that governed their territory long before they aspired to nationhood, whose major cities still name their parks and thoroughfares and hospitals after monarchs and battles of the imperial realm, and who have never managed to accept quite seriously the cultural claims of their putatively equal Francophones—what do such a people *mean*, even now, by national identity?

It is, as a Siamese monarch facing related questions is said once to have observed to Anna Leonowens of Halifax, Nova Scotia, a puzzlement.

The virtually obsessive fear of American hegemony Canadian nationalists express is not easily understood in the light of this apparent inconsistency. Hypersensitivity to economic control from abroad is not, to put it mildly, prominent in the Canadian tradition. A fundamental and familiar cause of the American Revolution was the American colonists' objection to British economic regulation and control—an objection which the loyal colonies to the north either failed to share or, in any case, regarded as insufficient cause for revolt. In the event, despite the persistent drain of Britain on their potential for economic growth, they decided not to seek the risks and responsibilities of revolution and self-rule. Nor can it be said that American exploitation of Canada has been more debilitating, in sheer economic terms, than British. American interests at least built those branch plants, while the British had been largely content to mine, trap, and harvest Canadian resources. The United States is, and long has been, Canada's best customer. It now accounts for about two-thirds of Canada's foreign trade, though a more independent Canada might have accrued still more from the same resources. In purely economic terms, that is, Canada has profited more, dollar for dollar, from its dealing with the United States than it has, dollar for pound, from its dealings with Britain—or, if you prefer, has been taken for less.

My point is not that economic exploitation of Canada by any other nation—or, for that matter, by the preemptive appropriation of Canada's resources for the enrichment of its own largely Anglo-Saxon elites—is justified, but that the Canadian sense of having suffered economic insult at American hands is both disproportionate to the injury sustained and a little out of character. Canada, as the Committee for an Independent Canada argues, is potentially one of the richest countries in the world—and not just in the long run when, as Maynard Keynes observed, we are all dead, but in the forseeable future. It can obviously afford to develop its own resources; in fact, it cannot afford not to. In a society with at least enough pretentions to social democracy that it cannot tolerate widespread, abject poverty, nothing is as inflationary as unemployment, which in Canada is both endemic and rife; for the value of a nation's currency is finally determined by the value of the goods and services it produces. Oil left undrilled this year may be produced in the next, but a man-hour of labor lost is wasted forever. Meanwhile, the idle body must be clothed and the clamorous mouth at least partly and intermittently filled, at whatever cost.

In terms of sheer and obvious economic self-interest, Canada ought long ago to have resorted to whatever deficit spending was necessary to pay for its own economic development, confident that the immediate inflationary effect would abate as the gross national product waxed abundant. It is quite true that Canada does not need to sell itself to foreign interests—British, American, or Oriental—in order to accomplish this. If it ever did need to, it certainly doesn't now.

The Canadian labor movement, also, has failed to evolve as

independently as Canadian nationalists would wish. Canadian social critics frequently complain of the domination of Canadian branches of international unions by their powerful American counterparts. This is a more difficult claim to assess than the corresponding complaint of economic domination by American corporate interests, both because it is harder to demonstrate conclusively and because it is less clear how the interests of the Canadian work force are or would be adversely affected even if it were true. One of the adverse consequences attributed to American influence is the failure of the labor movement in Canada (as in the United States) to develop a militant class consciousness like it has in Britain, and its willingness, instead, to limit its goals to traditional bread-and-butter issues instead of insisting on real political power and fundamental change in economic policy. But "big labor" in the United States, despite—or perhaps because of—its pragmatic, anti-ideological approach to power, seems to have much more political clout than Canadian labor despite a somewhat more favorable basic social climate in Canada. Socialism is not anathema to Canadians; the democratic-socialist New Democratic Party is frequently elected to power as a provincial government, though it has not yet managed to gain control at the federal level. Canadian labor legislation provides the usual protections for collective bargaining rights and labor practices, a reasonably high and fairly frequently adjusted minimum wage, and what have been until now generous provisions for unemployment benefits, by North American standards. No province has legislation comparable to the "right-to-work laws" by which unions are still weakened in some American states.

What keeps labor in Canada from becoming stronger politically? One major factor, clearly, is the same lack of fundamental rights that was discussed in the preceding chapter. One of the most basic pieces of American labor legislation is the provision in the Wagner Act, nearly half a century old, severely limiting the use of injunctions in labor disputes. There is no Canadian counterpart to this; the first thing Canadian employers do when faced with a strike is to turn to the courts to limit picketing, issue back-to-work orders, control the activities of organizers, and the like; and injunctive relief is often afforded them. Because

of the remoteness of many important sites of industrial development in Canada, there are still company towns that, in the event
of a strike, are simply closed down; the people who live in them
are summarily flown out, while persons who are not employed
are denied access to the community, which is wholly owned by
the developing corporation. When a strike involving some of the
employees of the huge James Bay hydroelectric development
project in the wilderness of northern Quebec happened to coin-
cide with the federal election of May 22, 1979, the striking employees lost their opportunity to vote. As soon as they struck,
the development corporation flew 650 of them to the small
town of Matagami, about 800 miles away. It stated that those
who wished to vote would be permitted to return for that purpose only—at a cost to themselves of about $200 for the round
trip. Quebec has probably the most progressive labor legislation
of any province in Canada, but it does not protect workers
against this kind of summary eviction from company property,
even when they reside there.

The absence of any constitutional protection against bills
of attainder or *ex post facto* legislation in Canada also weakens
labor unions—as, indeed, it must weaken any insurgent who
was relatively weak to begin with. The president of the Canadian
Union of Postal Workers, Jean-Claude Parrot, is currently appealing a jail sentence for "refusing to obey an Act of Parliament"
in the form of a special law ordering postal employees back to
work, although they had complied with the complex provisions
required for them to engage in a legal strike. Other officials of
the union were still awaiting trial as of May 1979. The judge
presiding in Mr. Parrot's case refused to allow the jury to hear
any evidence bearing on the strike or conditions in the post office itself; they were allowed to consider only whether he had,
in fact, ordered the members of his union back to work as Parliament had directed. The Canadian Labour Congress, which includes the CUPW, refused on this occasion to support the members or officials of the postal union, while Prime Minister Trudeau, in a campaign speech, rebuked protesting postal workers
at a rally for demanding "one law for union bosses and another
for the rest of us"; though to me, it seemed that this was just
what they were protesting against.

Faced with such custom and such precedent, union activity in Canada takes on a peculiar tone. Protest is likely to be angrier and more shrill than in the United States, but also—and justifiably—less confident. Canadians, fighting their status superiors on occasions when this cannot be avoided, are likely to sound like defiant children who have every reason to believe that, whether they are right or wrong, they are going to get spanked for being uppity. This is *not*, generally speaking, the way American Teamsters, in any of their manifold operations, respond; and their example must indeed be rather seductive to Canadians. But it cannot, surely, be an example that would tend to weaken them.

Dependency—economic, political and, in consequence, psychological—is common to the conflicts we have been discussing in this chapter, for it is a distinctive aspect of Canadian life. To declare that in Canada there have existed and shall continue to exist the economic resources necessary to an abundant life for its people is not to guarantee that the necessary political and, ultimately, psychological attitudes and predispositions also exist. At present they do not; they have never been developed in Canada. And it is this fact, I believe, which does most to explain and, indeed, to justify the rise of anti-American feeling in Canada. For what is feared is not just foreign domination but subversion of the Canadian identity and way of life by American hegemony. How else could Canadians feel about a neighbor so much larger, richer, stronger, and more aggressive? But what is feared, as I have said, is not just domination but *subversion*. American hegemony is more threatening to Canada than British or Japanese not only because it is now so much more immediate and powerful a threat, but because of differences in the two cultures, because of what the United States is and what Canada is. Americans, especially, have deceived themselves into believing that the two nations are far more similar culturally than they are. Most Americans, in fact, seem to believe either that Canada really is a part of the United States or that Canadians would think them rude if they said it wasn't—nobody likes to be reminded of past mistakes, even after two hundred years. If you think I exaggerate, try driving across the United States in an automobile with Canadian license plates and listen to what the gas attendant says when he fills out your charge slip, even though the Nova Scotia plate bears the legend, "Canada's Ocean Playground": "What state is that?" or, hopefully, "Is that near Bermuda?"

Nevertheless, in certain fundamental ways, the cousins are exceptionally ill-suited to each other, either because their qualities are antagonistic or because their mutual situation makes Canada exceptionally vulnerable to the United States. American interests do intervene in Canadian politics as they do in those of other countries; and American interests in Canada are usually more extensive. Executives of American branch plants, whether they are Canadian or American, are obviously dependent on decisions made in the United States for advancement to top-level slots. The RCMP and the CIA do each other's dirty work—but not in equal amounts. American economic policies, often undertaken without any thought of their effect on Canada, may weaken or destroy the economy of an entire community. And, of course, at this point in time, the top levels of power in the Western world are thought of as American when they are, at least nominally, international. Gordon Fairweather, one of the most imaginative and liberal-minded (though formally Progressive-Conservative) Canadian politicians, who resigned his seat in the House of Commons in 1977 to become chief comisioner of the newly formed Canadian Human Rights Commission, also became at about that time a member of the Trilateral Commission, an organization through which David Rockefeller and Zbigniew Brzezinski as *primii inter pares* formulate and define the problems of the Western World. The Trilateral Commission is not an American organization—it is called trilateral in reference to the presence on it of European members on one side, and gentlemen of Japan, their attitudes queer and quaint, on another—but it might as well be. Its meetings are reputedly even more fun than those of the Canadian Human Rights Commission; and membership on it is even stronger evidence of having made it. If it ever violated the human right of a Canadian, Mr. Fairweather might find himself in a situation of conflict; but it rarely if ever does such things. It's the top.

American hegemony over Canadian economics and politics is undoubtedly, then, partly a simple reflection of the facts of

current political and economic life. But it is also partly a consequence of the Canadian tradition of deference to authority,
which molded the attitudes of the Canadian ruling class through
the happy colonial years. Canadians, understandably and wisely,
don't like taking orders from Washington. But they do believe
in taking orders—sometimes quite unholy ones—from properly
authoritative sources. Washington pageantry tends to be a little
crude, though President Carter has at least stopped the military
bands from playing "Hail to the Chief" whenever he rears his
head; but if you want high-quality orders, that's where they
come from. You can't get anything comparable in Ottawa; nor
yet in London, though the Right Honorable Margaret Thatcher
is working on that.

The United States has no authority over Canada, it has
only power. But the essence of the colonial posture is that it
finds power self-legitimating, endowing it with authority in the
process of subjecting itself. Thus, Canada clings to the monarchy, declaring Elizabeth II to be head of state as queen of
Canada, not simply *ex officio* as queen of England; and the
monarchy retains important political functions. This fact is easily
misunderstood because the queen herself has no power—not
even to reject the advice of the ministers who nominally serve
her. But the reason she is deprived of power is no longer to preserve the liberties of her subjects, but to preserve the institution
itself from any apparent conflict and hence from disrespect, so
that when the people who *do* have power intend to make it
clear that they will brook no popular contradiction, they can
array themselves in its trappings. The ministers of the Crown
have power; the Crown prosecutor has power; and when a prime
minister or provincial premier and his party are obliged by political necessity to support legislation they do not really want
on the books, they need only ask the governor-general (or provincial lieutenant-governor) to delay proclaiming it in the queen's
name. It can't become law until he does. The Crown may rest
on the head of the sovereign, but its function is to cover the
government's arse.

In such a political system power tends to be even more self-
validating than usual. It always is, of course, to some degree; it
is essential to the stability of any political system that actual

political power, achieved and maintained, become recognized as legitimate authority. But in Canada the process almost doubles back on itself. It isn't just that the gaining of power leads to the granting of authority commensurate with it; one must somehow also be recognized as having been eligible all along. One can't just be admitted to the councils of state on one's own recognizance; one must be greeted and coopted as a long-lost elder brother who has regained his rightful, if previously unrecognized, status. The perils of an open society are thus averted, and coziness is maintained; the new member is no stranger, they just didn't realize he was there. If you have power, you *must* have authority, and if you aren't eligible, your actual power makes you an impostor, not just a rival and possible adversary or ally.

Americans are not only ineligible to have power over Canada; they gained that power in the first place by being disobedient. But the power cannot be ignored; it is real, and its effectiveness is enhanced by the Canadian habit of turning to the imperial center for validation. There has never been a time when a Canadian could gain superstar status by succeeding only in Canada; but as long as he could do so by making his reputation in Britain, no gross cultural incongruity was involved. New York and Los Angeles are a different matter, however. American hegemony, quite apart from its actual cultural content, is therefore a truly classic source of torment. It cannot be accepted and it cannot be ignored, while to resist it effectively requires a sharp break with the colonial tradition of identifying with the oppressor, which Canadian schools, courts, and politics continue to sustain. Canadian rage at what Americans do to Canada is therefore continually augmented by rage that it is Americans who are doing it.

But the actual cultural content, the specifically American content, also contributes to the subversive effect. American television is a persistent sore point with Canadian nationalists— though less so with Canadian viewers, apparently, since they continue to watch it in preference to Canadian programming when they have the choice. But it is difficult for those who wish to diminish the impact of American television on Canadian audiences to make practical recommendations for doing so. A majority of Canadians live close enough to the American border to be able to pick up American stations even if Canadian cable companies were prevented from carrying them; and about half the households in Canada do receive cable television—in developed areas like southern Ontario, far more than half. The Broadcasting Act that governs the licensing of radio and television broadcasting in Canada through the Canadian Radio-Telecommunications Commission states that the purpose of broadcasting in Canada—whether by the Canadian Broadcasting Corporation or privately owned companies—is to "safeguard, enrich, and strengthen the cultural, political, social and economic fabric of Canada." Unfortunately, what enriches the cultural fabric may weaken rather than strengthen the political, and what strengthens the political fabric may be economically debilitating.

At the periodic hearings which the CRTC holds pursuant to the renewal of licenses for Canadian broadcasting stations and networks, the licensee—especially in the case of the CBC—is warned to increase the Canadian and cut down the American content of its shows. During the past few years these warnings usually stressed establishing a minimum proportion of broadcast time to be devoted to Canadian material; for a time, 35 percent was regarded as an acceptable minimum, which seems low, but in the spring of 1979, the CRTC recommended that the CBC be urged to cut out American programming in prime time altogether except for special broadcasts of exceptional cultural significance. The CBC responded angrily that this sort of recommendation exceeded the authority of the CRTC, which is not supposed to prescribe or censor the content of programming and was, in any case, far more drastic than what had been asked of CTV, the private national network, a few months earlier—possibly in deference to the fact that CTV must be permitted to make money in order to stay in business, though CBC-TV also depends on advertising revenues to pay its operating expenses, since its government subsidy is inadequate for this purpose. At the time of this writing, the matter had not yet been resolved.

The CRTC, which grants cable companies a monopoly of service in their designated geographical area, but licenses them for only a year at a time, requires that non-Canadian material be assigned fifth and lowest priority in broadcasting, after CBC network material, private network material, material from Canadian independent stations, and local and educational programming from its own studios. The larger cable installations serving major metropolitan areas of Canada have enough channel capacity to do this and carry the American network programs, including public broadcasting, as well; and they do. Smaller cable companies omit one or more American networks, especially public broadcasting. Even in centers like Vancouver, strident conflicts arise when the CRTC attempts, as it recently did, to require the company to drop a popular American station to make room for the CBC's French-language programming, which few people in the Vancouver area can understand—though there is, indeed, a small Francophone community that has not been served.

It seems clear that there is nevertheless plenty of room on sets that are served by cable for both Canadian and American broadcasts. American TV shows do compete directly with Canadian productions for broadcast time on CBC and especially on CTV; it is cheaper to lease them than to produce material of comparable lavishness and technical quality. Many Canadians, especially those who are most concerned about problems of Canadian identity, argue that this is too important a matter to be determined by price, and that a nation which fails to insist on television programming that derives from and reflects its own values and patterns of life, relying instead on work, however meritorious, that conveys the culture of another people, is lost. They want American TV phased out of Canada, at any cost.

The cost would be high; and the problem is not, in any case, simple. What is Canadian content? Must the production be Canadian, or is it sufficient if the artists, producers, directors, or whoever are? Does it have to be made in Canada? Would it include films like *Days of Heaven*, *Superman*, or *McCabe and Mrs. Miller*, substantial portions of which were filmed in Canada, though the scenes shot there are depicted as American? How are calculations to be affected by the tendency of Canadian artists who want to make it big to seek their fortunes south of the border and the reluctance of Canadians to concede that they have made it big unless they do? But difficult as it might be to devise a formula determining what to count as Canadian content, one could obviously be worked out arbitrarily and imposed—and will be, if there is enough political pressure to do it.

But if this is done to safeguard the cultural, political, social, and economic fabric of Canada, it will certainly not enrich it; and I doubt also that it will ultimately strengthen it. This is a difficult issue to debate, for several reasons. The most important of these is that the precise nature of the impact of TV on its audiences has not been clearly established even yet. The evidence does tend to suggest that the actual content of the programs viewed may be less important than the context of viewing: the passivity, the spurious sense of participation, the acceptance of the indignity of continual interruption by sales pitches of various kinds—and these, whatever their effects, are the common conditions of both American and Canadian television.

Nevertheless, the content does matter; and it is the content of American television that Canadians who object to it find subversive of Canadian culture and Canadian identity. It certainly conflicts with elements of both. But conflict strenthens what it does not overwhelm; and American culture is rich in just those elements in which Canadian culture is crucially deficient. Even some of the worst features of American culture, as reflected in its television, might invigorate Canadian life in small doses. There is doubtless too much violence on American TV and in American life, as Canadians complain; there is much less in Canada, especially in life. There is, perhaps, too little. Violence in public affairs is usually deplorable; but it should not be unthinkable.

There are other themes in American television whose potential contribution to Canadian life is less easily contested. In my first chapter I mentioned the anger I had heard expressed that Canadian youngsters were picking up from American TV shows the idea that they had civil liberties which Canadians, in fact, do not possess. If that is subversion, Canada should be grateful for it—not for the confusion, but for the notice of deficiency. Usually, though, what is involved is less factual and somewhat more subtle. When the CRTC announced its recent recommendation that the CBC stop broadcasting regular American series in prime time, two of the shows the CBC carried and defended as worth carrying—though both would be lost if the recommendation is upheld by the Crown corporation's governing board—were *The White Shadow* and *Barney Miller*. Each of these illustrates quite specifically what I have in mind. Neither is great drama; both are sentimental and sometimes grossly and offensively so, and in ways that are by no means harmless or negligible. *The White Shadow* softens the hard edges of racial antagonism in the United States and is quite conformist beneath its liberal facade. *Barney Miller* makes New York's Finest far more lovable than they are; precinct houses are not cozy places in New York any more than—or, at least, not much more than —in Toronto.

But *The White Shadow*, whatever it may lack in fidelity to social fact in its portrayal of a white basketball coach dedicated to his mostly black highschool team, does portray the relationship between them as genuinely conflict-laden, with faults, rights, and a sense of dignity on both sides. The coach does not regard the team as a set of problems to be rehabilitated; in fact, some of the program's best sequences involve his struggles against and capitulations to the school's superliberal guidance personnel. This recalls the issue raised by the *Canadian Forum*'s review of *Outrageous!* quoted in chapter 1. And the boys on the team are never pictured as merely rebellious, though often as disobedient. They have purposes, values, and sometimes minds of their own. They do wrong and usually get into trouble for it —*The White Shadow* is often offensively moralistic—but when they do, it is because their actions were foolish, impractical, or reprehensible, not because they were disobedient. Authority, as such, is not an issue in this series; it is assumed that poor, black highschool kids will have no respect for authority and no reason to respect it—though they are portrayed as having respect for themselves and one another and even, when he deserves it, for their coach. The program also avoids the alternative danger of sentimentalizing blacks as such; the school principal and most of the faculty are black, and vary from decent and reasonably honest in the case of the principal to truly awful and pretentious, as any such group would be likely to vary. None of this is a big deal; they cause problems, but the program doesn't reify them into a social problem themselves. Compare all this to the desperate high school boy who, when he is finally goaded into dropping out of school by harsh and uncomprehending teachers in the National Film Board of Canada's much praised *No Reason to Stay*, fantasizes that his defection is front-page news and that the prime minister, reading of it, observes sadly, "This is bad for the country."

Barney Miller, with its anthology of lovably ethnic detectives—a black, a Pole, a pedantic young German and, until he died in real life, a Japanese, captained by a patient Jew—is more patently hung up in liberal stereotypy, from which it usually redeems itself by genuine and humane wit. But its view of the law as itself a social problem and comically errant; its sympathy for the guile and malice in the criminals Miller's force tries to deal with; its pride in the utter lack of spit and polish and its utter nonviolence—all this is unique in police shows. *Barney Miller* is so devoid of paranoia you could call it orthonoiac. It is also a very valuable corrective to a society that still regards the RCMP police barracks in Regina, where postulants to the force are sent for training and where Louis Riel was hanged in 1885, much as good Catholics regard the shrine at Lourdes: they agree that it has been subject to abuse by the credulous and ignorant, and they are somewhat skeptical about it themselves, but it keeps the faithful together and they're glad to have it there when they need it.

American popular culture embodies and conveys a number of social attitudes that are much rarer in Canadian popular culture. Most Canadians would not only agree that this is true but express heartfelt gratitude for the rarity. But I would argue that what is worst about American culture is far more easily accepted in Canada than what is best; and in this respect the damage has already been done. While many Canadians doubtless feel that Heather Robertson, in observing in her regular column in the April 1975 issue of *Maclean's* magazine, "I confess to a desire to toss a hand grenade into every American camper I pass on the highway," herself exceeded the bounds of good taste, they might also argue that her comment simply demonstrated the degree to which the unfortunate woman, like so many of her compatriots, had succumbed to American influence already. Perhaps so, indeed: *The Silent Partner*, released in 1979, is one of the most chilling crime films made in the past few years, and skillfully exploits its Toronto setting, whose stuffiness and sexual hypocrisy provides the essential context of the tale. The icy glitter of Toronto should be a welcome sight to North American audiences after their improbable encounters with the likes of Sylvester Stallone and Glenda Jackson in Philadelphia recently, and the cloying *pseudogemeinschaft* of Mary Tyler Moore's Minneapolis. Minneapolis is further north than Toronto and a lot colder; but it lacks Toronto's *sangfroid*, which *The Silent Partner* captures and which rivals Truman Capote's.

So violence, I think, is no longer a distinctively American rather than Canadian theme; nor is consumerism, which is another trait Canadians tend to attribute more readily to Americans than to themselves. I wish it were still possible to get a discussion going on this point between Ernest Hemingway and, say, Morley Callaghan, to carry on where Scott Fitzgerald left off: "Americans are different from us." "Yes, they have more money." Well, Canadians are certainly different from Americans but not, I think, in the innate modesty of their patterns of consumption. Canadian commercials are as blatant or more than American commercials and often in especially offensive ways: the continual portrayal of women as sex objects intended solely for the delight of males and perpetually impeded in fulfilling their mission by their displeasing natural odor; and of children whose cutesy condition and peculiar piping speech suggests that lobotomy, or worse, must be routine procedure in Canadian pediatric hospitals. Canadian women's rights organizations have recently launched serious complaints about their degradation in TV commercials but have so far been given a polite run-around. The children, who have equal cause, have not organized to protest and their parents, by and large, would be either condescendingly amused if they did or angered at their impertinence.

Similar offensive commercials doubtless abound on American television; but there is much more in the medium to countervail against them. Paternalism, a powerful and malign social force in Canada, is not a theme American audiences as easily find sympathetic, though the media in both countries willingly give law 'n' order more than its due. *Hawaii Five-O*, for example —which the CBC carries and which is consistently racist, sexist, and deferential to constituted authority—is worse than anything Canadian TV would be likely to dream up, for Canadians are now even further into liberalism than Americans and less likely to portray criminals simply as bad guys whose misdeeds are both asocial and apolitical. (The CBC, if it had the power, would long ago, I suspect, have turned *Hawaii Five-O* into a documentary about racial tensions, poverty, and pollution in an American tropical paradise, though the governor and police would still be presented as a source of white hope.) But American audiences, precisely because they are turned on to and accept media brutality, have less need to portray authority as basically decent and protective. The treatment of basically political themes in the American media is unlikely to achieve the searching candor of a neo-Marxist critique—though in the event, *The China Syndrome* proved an adequate and even prescient documentary—but American films and to a lesser degree American TV are far more likely to be candid about crude and basic political and economic motivations and the deformations of character associated with them. The dominant North American capitalist economy is not apt to provide the kinds of accounts of the sociopolitical-economic-military-industrial process that will lead to effective demystification. But Americans do raise some of the right questions, directly or by implication, even when they fail to provide a schematic that would lead to the insights which would be useful. Canadian popular culture avoids— I should say sedulously—even suggesting that the questions can be raised outside a formal documentary format where the controls are solidly built in. Within these limits, it surpasses American TV: programs that focus sharply on cases or issues one at a time, like the CBC's *Ombudsman*, *Marketplace*, and *The Watson Report*, have been admirable in providing media exposure of specific abuses and sometimes unforgettable vignettes of the Canadian politician under scrutiny. But they have no mythic quality; or rather, the little they do have makes matters worse by continually suggesting that, though bullies will be bullies, the nursery is defended by wise observers after all.

Paternalism also forms the basis for the maintenance of racism in Canadian society, which, like American, is formally committed to equal treatment of all persons regardless of ethnicity—even Americans. And, indeed, Canadian society is less plagued by hostilities between ethnic groups than is American society. Orientals have never fared well in Canada, and the construction of the Canadian Pacific Railway—like that of the Central Pacific to the south—cost many Chinese lives. But overt, lethal, racist violence has not figured large in Canadian history or, for that matter, in Canadian attitudes. Harriet Beecher Stowe did indeed visit Josiah Henson, the prototype of Uncle Tom, in the Ontario village to which he had fled as a runaway slave; he had established a fugitive-slave settlement there and had become the pastor of its Methodist church.

Economic rivalries fueled the intensity of bitterness between ethnic groups in the United States because, among other reasons, the stakes were always so great and the grasp of privilege, though viselike, lacked the sanction of custom as well as of law. Henry Ford, that arch-American of his time, was an embittered racist and propagator of the infamous *Protocols of the Elders of Zion*. It is possible that, among the torments he now doubtless endures, is the awareness that American cosmopolitan culture has become fundamentally Jewish, while the head of the Ford Foundation is a BASP. Americans differ in the degree to which they take pride in these developments; some remain displeased. But none thinks it strange; the country s'pozed to work like that, even if it usually doesn't. In Canada, it seems very strange indeed, even though the exploitation of ethnic minorities, common to both countries, has been more usually cloaked in benevolence here, and violence has been restrained by the law-and-order trappings of the Northwest Mounted Police, whose spokesmen—though off the record—make no bones about the fact that the RCMP is still a WASP organization.

For in Canada there has never been any doubt about whose culture was most authoritative and whose authority most cultured. The British ruling classes have never hated lesser breeds beyond the law and are embarrassed to discover how very cross the British working class has become about shouldering its share of the White Man's Burden. Proper British, and proper Canadians, treat foreigners and those not naturally Anglophone as children. Unfortunately, they don't respect children very much, feel not only free but morally obligated to lie to them for the sake of peace, order, and good government, and grow very angry indeed if the children catch them at it and demand more equal treatment, as promised. Anger has gone out of fashion—though it is still publicly displayed in response to "back talk" in Canada; for example, both Mr. Trudeau and Mr. Clark, in the spring 1979 federal election campaign, publicly accused those who raised embarrassing questions in open meetings (the Canadian press calls this heckling) of having been hired to do so; they treated this accusation as self-evident, requiring no proof and no answer. More commonly, the demand for equal respect is treated with patronizing indulgence as further and conclusive evidence of immaturity. Let me again refer to Cam Hubert's *Dreamspeaker* for a tragic exegesis of this state of mind.

What the American media can contribute and what Canadian society sorely needs, then, is a different way of looking at authority as a factor in human interaction and as an essential though dangerous political device. It is too much to expect them to provide an alternative way of looking at society and its basic political arrangements; the fact that, to Canadian eyes, the American system is itself such an alternative, and a very seductive one, is finally what makes American media penetration subversive. But this resistance, understandable as it may be, is beside the point. Canada doesn't want the American political system, doesn't need it, and couldn't make it work. But life in Canada could be made much freer, and political institutions more stable, if Canadians could get the message that is already grasped at some level by most Americans: that authority is, in every sense, inherently questionable, and that protection which denies respect is no protection at all.

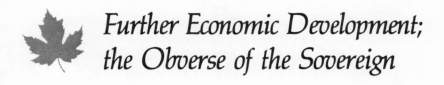

6

Further Economic Development; the Obverse of the Sovereign

Previous sections of this book have been concerned with various ways in which the liberties of Canadians are restricted and infringed by governmental authority. In fact, Canadians appear to possess no formal liberties conceived to lie beyond the scope of legitimate government intervention. Formal guarantees of liberty are not absolute, of course, even when they are explicit. All governments violate their own constitutional guarantees under extraordinary circumstances; but they vary greatly in how seriously those guarantees are taken, and in how extraordinary those circumstances have to be. Even governments that regard themselves as seriously committed to maintaining the liberties of their people differ widely in how precisely those liberties are set forth, how freely the government may determine what constitutes a threat sufficient to justify their abridgment, and how subject its executive decision then is to criticism and review.

Canada, I have argued, ranks low on these indices of liberty, while the Canadian public is generally too complaisant to demand more freedom of it. If eternal vigilance be the price of liberty, Canada faces—with disturbing equanimity—the continuous threat of foreclosure. Yet, in reaching this conclusion, I have so far emphasized legal restrictions on freedom. This leaves some very important issues unfaced.

In the United States the Constitution is a very serious part of the machinery of government; it has proved remarkably— though far from perfectly—successful in limiting the power of the government of the United States to intrude upon its own nationals. Americans have, of course, been able to afford this scrupulousness in no small measure because we have been able to intrude more freely and profitably on the lives of hundreds of millions of nationals of other countries—Canada among them—whom our Constitution does not protect. But American self-satisfaction at having devised so self-limiting a system of government makes us easily mystified as to how people—including ourselves—are ultimately governed.

Most of the policies and actions that mold and limit our lives do not originate in state agencies, but with what we still regard as private (though usually corporate) entities. Even when these use the government as their instrument, they often do so in ways that cannot be challenged effectively in the courts; for their victims are not their targets, and hence have no legal standing to resist them. The victims just happen to be living in the wrong place, at the wrong time, in the wrong line of activity. Their livelihood is lost; they can no longer afford what they need to go on living; or the poisons seeping into their basements from abandoned chemical wastes have, in any case, limited their option to do so, though no one may have informed them of the risk. But their liberties have not been threatened.

Freedom is less often the victim of tyranny than of casualty; and actions that deprive people of it, when they result from corporate policies, are not conceived as attacks on liberty at all. Neither in Canada nor in the United States does the Bill of Rights as such apply to transactions in which the government plays no part. It also follows, at least in principle, that since the most significant threats to liberty are extragovernmental in origin, liberty may on balance be safer in a country such as Canada which lacks effective formal, legal safeguards than in one like the United States which provides them. Canadians may have been slow to adopt these constraints on government action because they have less need of them; and they may have less need of them because they derive protection from a greater balance among private and public sources of power than in the United States. Perhaps for these or other reasons they have less need of formal guarantees. We do not call the citizens of Calcutta improvident because their municipal government spends so little on snowplows. Though we do notice that, even among the inhabitants of that City of Dreadful Night, there are those who are both young and rich enough to fly to the hills, or even to Switzerland, when they want to go skiing.

Certainly the threat of domination by corporate power has been considered serious in Canada for a very long time—as long as in the United States, indeed, slightly longer.

> In 1889, the Canadian government enacted the predecessor to the present Combines Investigation Act, predating the Sherman Act in the United States by a year. This legislation reflected concern over both the growing size of corporations and potential abuses of corporate power, such as restrictive practices, by some large firms.

This quotation is taken from page 1 of the *Report of the Royal Commission on Corporate Concentration*, submitted to the governor-general in council in March 1978. The appointment of the commission by order-in-council on May 1, 1975, seems conclusive evidence that such a concern existed, and has continued to exist until the present era.

The *Report* cannot be called alarmist in tone; and it seems unlikely that the three commissioners who produced it were shocked by what they found. The chairman of the commission was Robert B. Bryce, who resigned for health reasons after two years—and after the commission's "research work and public hearings" had been completed and it had, according to its *Report*, "made considerable progress on crystallizing our views and drafting this *Report*." Bryce was described by Peter Newman in volume 1 of *The Canadian Establishment** as "the quintessential mandarin, a pervasive Ottawa behind-the-scenes influence as clerk of the privy council, as deputy minister of finance, and later as chairman of the Royal Commission on Corporate Concentration." Bryce was appointed executive director of the International Monetary Fund in 1971. The deputy-commissioner was Pierre A. Nadeau, president, chief executive officer, director, and chairman of the board of Petrofina Canada, Ltd., the Belgian-controlled oil company that at the time was Canada's sixth largest petroleum firm. M. Nadeau is also a director of the Royal Bank, Canada's largest. The third commissioner, Robert W. V. Dickerson of Vancouver, is not listed in the *Canadian*

---

*(Toronto: McClelland and Stewart, 1975), p. 332.

Who's Who—an indication, perhaps, of the commission's breadth of scope—but it seems safe to assume, in the absence of evidence to the contrary, that he is not and has never been a member of the Communist Party of Canada. The *Report*, it is fair to note, does mention having received and considered a brief from the latter organization.

One might argue that the power of the governor-in-council to select and appoint such an investigating commission to dispose of public concern about the concentration of corporate power in Canada is already enough to answer the basic questions about this matter more eloquently than any subsequent report could hope to. And indeed, in this respect, the commission remains true to itself as Polonius might have wished. It is no apologist for the interests of large corporations; it would not have occurred to it that any apology is necessary. The tone of the report is marvelously represented in the following passage dealing with the possible reciprocal influences between corporate policy and national foreign policy. The commission notes that

> during the 1960s Canada's foreign policy called for condemnation of apartheid in South Africa, and for foreign aid to increase the standard of living in the Caribbean region; but during this period the sugar industry in Canada switched its procurement of raw sugar from the Caribbean countries to South Africa. However, there has been no systematic study of the problem, no indication that the individual cases took place without the knowledge of the Canadian government and no publicly available information about other considerations that may have been seen by the government as offsetting the implied "harms." In addition, it is often difficult to say what the foreign or any other "policy" of the Canadian or any other government is, and even more difficult to test particular conduct or action against it. A government "policy" is often no more than the expression of a hope or sentiment, and a particular policy or an aspect of it frequently conflicts with another. It will seldom be possible to draw useful conclusions about corporate social responsibility by weighing a corporation's actions against government policy.*

Earlier, the commission had commented:

Several Canadian corporations testified before us that their policy

*Report of the Royal Commission on Corporate Concentration, pp. 374-75.

was to consider business operations in each individual country on their own economic and social merits unless it was explicit Canadian government policy that they not participate. This seems to us the proper approach to this problem.*

The complacency of the Royal Commission on Corporate Concentration tends, in certain ways, to enhance its usefulness for our purposes, especially in view of the commission's conscientiousness. It worked hard and, within its ideological limits, intelligently. It received and considered more than 200 written briefs from all over the country and from a wide range of individuals and organizations, skewed toward the corporate side but still covering the whole political spectrum; the only startling omission is the lack of any brief from an organization representing the interests of native people in Canada. (The *Report*, in fact, ignores the fate and interests of Canada's original inhabitants altogether, though these are the people who have been most affected by the thrust of economic power in Canada.) The commission held three rounds of public hearings from November 3, 1975, till September 13, 1976, gathering 8,000 pages of transcript from 127 witnesses. It commissioned and published thirty-three specialized research monographs on particular corporations and on special problem areas. The scope and quality of the commission's work, it seems to me, combine with its unconcealed ideological bias to make its criticisms and warnings about possible malfunctions of the Canadian corporate structure very convincing—few and temperate though they are. These men, and most of the witnesses they heard, are disinclined to find fault with the present distribution of power in Canada. When they nevertheless do conclude that a problem may exist, it does.

The commission is also led into candor by the very strength of its commitment to the world of corporate power; it is not at all defensive about how the system works and is quite lucid about its operation, where a mere corporate flack would be cagey. It does not, certainly, blink at the fact of concentrated corporate power as such. The commission concedes—affirms? boasts?—that "aggregate concentration is higher in Canada than in the United States" (p. 11) and "industrial concentration

*Ibid., p. 346.

in Canada is substantially higher than in comparable industries in the United States" (p. 12). This is true even though "the average size of Canada's 100 largest non-financial corporations and the average size of Canada's 25 largest financial corporations are very much smaller than the average size of their counterparts in the United States and other developed countries" (p. 11). Canadian ducks, in short, are not very big as ducks go; but they are enormous, and few, for the size of the Canadian puddle. This is generally true throughout Canadian industry. As judged from the proportion of the market covered by the top four firms in each industry in both Canada and the United States,

> in 50 of 56 comparable industries Canadian concentration levels for 1948 were significantly higher than the 1947 levels in the United States. A comparison prepared by the Department of Consumer and Corporate Affairs of Canadian concentration levels in 1965 with U.S. data for 1963 and 1966 revealed similar results: of the 116 manufacturing industries in the sample, 98 were significantly more concentrated in Canada. A more recent comparison prepared by the Conference Board of Canada using 1972 concentration levels supports the previous finding that concentration is higher in Canada than in the United States. More specifically, roughly twice as many industries in Canada had 4-firm concentration levels in excess of 60%.
>
> Since 1945, official concentration data for individual manufacturing industries have been published in a number of countries on a more or less regular basis. A sample of nine Canadian manufacturing industries with similarly defined counterpart industries in other foreign countries was selected. They are slaughtering and meat processing, breweries, tobacco products manufacturing, rubber tire and tube manufacturing, pulp and paper mills, iron and steel mills, motor vehicle manufacturing, cement manufacturing and petroleum refining. These industries are relatively easy to identify; moreover, they represent the largest Canadian manufacturing industries. We collected concentration data for these industries from several sources . . . . This international comparison of industrial concentration ratios indicated that concentration in Canada is higher than in the other countries studied (including the United States, West Germany, France, Japan and Sweden). In particular, concentration in Canada is higher than in the United States for *all nine sample industries*.* [Emphasis added]

"It is well established," the commission concludes, "by

*Ibid., pp. 39-40.

several independent studies using data for several different years, that industrial concentration in Canada is higher than in the United States. The weight of the evidence on this point is sufficient to treat this as an established empirical fact" (p. 42). Less conclusively, the commission also infers that "the trend of the evidence suggests that concentration in Canada is higher than in other industrial countries, even those with economies of roughly the same size" (p. 42).

Today, of course, it seems that nearly every individual in the world feels himself besieged by giant, impersonal forces from which he can evoke no response. Is Canada, too, then— that land noted for quiet, privacy, and isolation—one more recent victim of the creeping economic concentration that threatens to enslave small men everywhere? It seems not. For the commission states as its very first "major empirical finding":

> Aggregate concentration (i.e. the percentage of economic activity accounted for by the largest firms in Canada) *decreased* from 1923 to 1975; however, the greatest portion of this decrease took place before 1966. Since 1966, aggregate concentration in Canada has changed very little. [emphasis added]

In Canada, there has existed and will continue to exist, extreme concentration of economic power. But this fact of itself does not tell us how that concentration affects the quality of life in Canada or the freedom of individual Canadians, and these are much more complex questions. They must be approached obliquely, and in the light of a variety of additional factors. It seems reasonable, first, to ask whether this high concentration of economic power in Canada is accompanied by an unusual measure of constraint as well; that is, whether entrepreneurs in Canada enjoy an unusual degree of protection from competition and from the annoying demands of consumers and environmentalists, beyond that afforded by their sheer size and oligarchic position.

They do—and have since longer than Canada has been a country. The first formal political entity to be called, simply, Canada was a province formed by Act of Union of the British Parliament in 1841—the first of a so far unending series of none-too-satisfactory attempts to combine Ontario and Quebec under a single government acceptable to both. In 1859—still eight years before confederation—the minister of finance of the colony, Alexander Galt, introduced the first industrial tariff in Canada, designed to protect fledgling industry from competition. Even Britain accepted it, after suitable protest. In fact, Galt was a little late; in 1857, anticipating a device that, within a century, would come to dominate the Canadian economy, a Massachusetts distiller named Hiram Walker moved to Canada West (Ontario) and evaded any such possible control by establishing his plant there.*

In 1879, the Conservative government of Canada's first prime minister, Sir John A. Macdonald, enacted what came to be known as "the National Policy," which the *Oxford Companion to Canadian History and Literature* characterizes as "a euphemism that softened a return to the system of protective tariff," which the Liberal interregnum under Alexander Mackenzie had treated as a source of revenue instead of protection. Protectionism has been an established—though controversial—Canadian economic policy ever since: "for more than one hundred years Canada has attempted to foster a national market for Canadian manufacturers by means of a high (though lowering) tariff wall." † In this context, the commission's use of the adjective "lowering" is ambiguous; presumably, the intended meaning is threatening and gloomy.

There is, of course, nothing unusual about Canada's use of tariff protection to encourage the growth of national industry. What seems to me significant about it is the celerity with which Canadians turned to this solution, placing the interests of manufacturers above those of consumers from the very outset, and never seriously considering that they might emerge the victors in an open competition with their American and British rivals. In a sense, this position might be thought to have been adumbrated by the acceptance in the loyal northern colonies of the restraints imposed on trade by the British Crown—restraints that played a large role in driving their southern counterparts to revolt. Free trade early became a controversial issue in the United

*Clement Wallace, *The Canadian Corporate Elite* (Toronto: McClelland and Stewart, 1975), p. 62.
†*Report of the Royal Commission on Corporate Concentration*, p. 43.

States, too. South Carolina created a constitutional crisis in 1828 by claiming the right to nullify by state legislation what it called a federal "tariff of abominations"; it lost, though it got the tariff reduced. The issue, never finally resolved, increasingly divided the nation as its economy developed. But the United States never came to rely on protectionism as Canada did, or as it might have, if it had had a rich, pushy neighbor ten times as populous as itself.

The effect of Canada's high-tariff policy on the lives and freedom of its people is difficult to assess. It certainly keeps the cost of living higher than it otherwise would be—about a third higher, on the whole, than in regions with comparable demographic conditions in the States, I would judge, though this varies a lot at different times and places as well as with different goods and services, and with differences in the inflation rates in the two countries. Even when the Canadian dollar is worth more than the American dollar—as it sometimes is, on money markets—it won't buy as much, which seems, to the naive mind, peculiar. Not all of this is due to trade barriers, of course; it has become customary to place part of the blame on higher production and distribution costs occasioned by the relatively small size of the Canadian market and scattered population. This is undoubtedly a factor in serving remote parts of the country; but "most Canadians live within 100 miles of the U.S. border (16 of the 21 cities of more than 100,000 population are located there). . . . Sixty percent of the total is concentrated in a 600-mile strip between Quebec City and Windsor, Ontario, in less than two percent of the country's area."* For these people, the costs of exclusion from the American production and distribution network are considerable—high enough, in fact, that when the two currencies are close to par, Vancouver residents find it cheaper to drive across the border to shop in Bellingham, Washington, about forty miles away, and pay duty on what they bring back from the supermarket—customs hassles and all. What Canadians gain, presumably, is increased job opportunities in plants that might not be there without the protection of tariffs and import quotas. Or that might be there, if they had

The Canadian Pocket Encyclopedia, 33rd ed. (Toronto: Quick Canadian Facts Limited, 1978-79), p. 2.

learned to operate more efficiently. Or that might have been replaced with other and greater employment opportunities, if
prices had been lower and the economy correspondingly more
dynamic.

At any rate, it seems clear that most Canadians live in areas
that are densely urban enough to be serviced as economically as
are most parts of the United States. The companies that serve
them are *much* smaller than their American counterparts, and
Canadian industrial plants tend to be too small to be optimally
efficient, but not in all industries. Data on this point are complicated and conflicting, and derived in some cases from studies
that may be out of date. Taking all this into account, the Commission on Corporate Concentration concludes:

> Undoubtedly Canadian plants in many industries are smaller than
> those in other countries. But . . . when the low end of the plant size
> distribution is excluded, Canadian plants are not, in general, very
> much smaller. The fact that the Canadian market is only one-tenth
> the size of the U.S. market does not imply that industrial plants in
> Canada are one tenth the size of the U.S. plants as well. Plant-spe-
> cific economies of scale, what have been the main focus of most of
> the studies, are significant in a few Canadian industries but have not,
> in general, imposed a major cost disadvantage on Canadian firms
> serving the Canadian market.*

The *Report* goes on to point out, however, that

> to compete with imports and to satisfy consumer demand, Canadian
> firms in tariff-protected oligopolies produce . . . a much more diver-
> sified line of products than do similar-sized plants in the United
> States . . . employ less specialized equipment, have a higher propor-
> tion of set-up and downtime, and experience fewer of the economies
> of scale that arise from "learning by doing."

Protectionism clearly costs the Canadian consumer a lot in
standard of living and in product choice. But many Canadians
argue that this may be a very good thing, insofar as it is a factor
in protecting Canadian society from the evils of rampant American consumerism. Restrictions of access to the Canadian market are justified not merely in terms of economic necessity but

---

*Report of the Commission on Corporate Concentration, p. 67.

primarily in cultural terms—as helping to protect Canada at least a little from the waves that continually inundate it from the south and leave its shores polluted with the detritus of American culture. Like restrictions on advertising on American TV stations and on American content in TV programs, trade restrictions are thought to retard the destructive onslaught of Americanization.

But the cultural consequences are complex and ambiguous. Economic policies that leave a people without as much to choose from in the marketplace or the means to pay for it if they find it *do* seem un-American, but they probably do not lower the value placed on consumer goods any more than sexual isolation has tended to encourage an attitude of diffidence and respect toward women among sailors in the Royal Navy. Even if protectionism fails to make Canadians less avid consumers than Americans, however, by impairing the means rather than the desire, it might still be a productive policy in cultural terms if it fosters the development of a distinctively *Canadian* market and hence a *Canadian* life-style instead of a watered-down Americanism. Does it?

In some ways, yes; in some ways, no. Again, the question is complex, the answers ambiguous.

The most immediate, conspicuous, and probably influential consequence of Canadian protectionism has been the proliferation of American branch-plant enterprise. In chapter 5, I mentioned the so-called Gray Report, published in 1972 under the title *Foreign Direct Investment in Canada*. Its principal author, the Honorable Herb Gray, member of Parliament for Windsor West since 1962 and minister of national revenue at the time the Gray Report was prepared, resigned from the cabinet in 1974 and remained a back-bencher for five years. In July 1979, after the defeat of his party in the general election held earlier that year, he was named finance critic in the opposition shadow cabinet. Gray has one of the finest financial minds of any Canadian statesperson—a fact that apparently restored him to Mr. Trudeau's favor after the Liberal defeat insured that Gray's critical faculties would be directed at the Opposition rather than at his Liberal colleagues. Seven years later, the Gray Report remains the most cogent analysis of the implications and

consequences of foreign—principally American—direct investment in Canada. It stresses the stultifying consequences of foreign domination rather than the exploitive ones. The Canadian
polity is harmed less by being drained than by being kept in a
state of arrested development, so that top-level research and
managerial functions are simply truncated. In good times, the
Canadian economy is impressively bushy, but it doesn't blossom
on top. Resources are developed, probably faster than they could
be without extensive foreign investment—though Canada's
banks might well do it if they were willing to try, and the banks
are Canadian—but not in correspondence with Canada's needs.
Public revenues are ripped off by the practice of feeding the less
profitable operations to Canadian subsidiaries to save on higher
Canadian taxes. Canadian firms, of course, do a lot of this sort
of thing in turn by maintaining branch plants in Brazil, the
Caribbean, and more remote parts of the industrially underde-
veloped world. But most Canadian direct foreign investment is
in the United States. Canadian direct investment abroad totaled
nearly $11 billion in 1975—a little over half of it in the United
States.* U.S. direct investment abroad in the same year was
about $125 billion, with over $30 billion in Canada.† On the
basis of these figures, Canadian direct investment in the United
States ran about two-thirds higher per capita than American direct investment in Canada, though the impact on the Canadian
economy was far greater.

About a third of Canada's industrial capital is invested
from abroad,‡ and more than three-quarters of that comes from
the United States, which surpassed Britain as the major foreign
investor in Canada in the postwar boom of the 1920s; the American contribution now seems to have leveled off at about 30
percent of capital invested in Canadian industry and may be declining slightly.§ But it is arguable that American influence on
Canadian industry has always been greater than British because,
ever since confederation, U.S. *direct* investment has been greater
than British. British investment in Canada has been largely port-

*Statistics Canada, *Canada Year Book 1978-79*, p. 855.

†*The World Almanac*, 1978, p. 75.

‡Statistics Canada, op. cit., p. 856.

§Ibid., p. 856; Clement, op. cit., p. 384.

folio investments, and bondholders and preferred stockholders don't vote, while parent holding companies directly control the policies of their foreign-based subsidiaries. Except during the two world wars and the interegnum between them, U.S. direct investment has also been larger than U.S. portfolio investment in Canada. "The introduction of $6.107 billion dollars in U.S. direct investment alone between 1952 and 1960 is almost twice the total of all U.K. investment present in Canada at any point in history."* "The U.S.—that replaced the U.K. as Canada's principle source of imports in 1876 and as her principal market for exports in 1920—now accounts for some 70 per cent of Canada's total trade."† Except during wartime, when the Canadian economy as a whole was stringently administered by the government, these developments have been subjected to little governmental regulation until quite recently. Wartime foreign exchange controls were repealed in 1952, though the decline of the Canadian economy and increasingly unfavorable Canadian balance of trade continually raises the specter of possible reimposition. Probably because the British North America Act reserves jurisdiction over "property and civil rights" to the provinces rather than to the federal government, and the provinces jealously defend this prerogative, the federal government has been reluctant to act directly on questions of ownership of property. The federal Foreign Investment Review Agency, which now controls acquisition or establishment of businesses in Canada by non-Canadians, became effective on April 9, 1974.

In view of these facts, it becomes difficult to understand how the Canadian economy and the society that depends on it have remained as distinctive as they are, and why they continue to insist desperately on defending an independence that has long since been compromised. This continued defiance of the American presence and the laws of probability is especially striking in view of the fact that the policies of the Canadian government, especially when the Liberal party is in power, have tended to favor continentalism—that is, freerer trade among the peoples of North America, especially those who speak English clearly enough to make their desires understood—and the expansion

*Clement, op. cit., p. 118; see also p. 384.

†*The Canadian Pocket Encyclopedia*, p. 98.

of American interests. Many Canadians, especially those with leftish political leanings, would feel that I have expressed the matter too delicately. Many Canadian officials are, and have been, Macdonalds—though the Big Mac himself was not a Liberal—which may explain why they have so often responded to American clients by asking whether they would rather take Canada home or eat it here.

Excessive deference to American investment demands, in fact, precipitated the downfall of Liberal Party government in 1957, after twenty-two years in office. The debacle was brought about through the intransigence of one of the most singular and surely most despotic individuals ever to hold public office in Canada—Clarence Decatur Howe. American-born and educated at the Massachusetts Institute of Technology, Howe became Canada's economic czar during the 1940s as director of the Wartime Industries Control Board. His powers continued unabated —and his arrogance apparently grew—as a cabinet minister in the postwar Liberal government of Louis St. Laurent, the downfall of which is generally attributed to the "Pipeline Scandal" (someday, doubtless, to be known as the First Pipeline Scandal) Howe created. In order to secure $70 million in government funds for the construction of a pipeline that would cross the Canadian prairies but was designed to serve consumers in the American Midwest, Howe in 1956 induced a compliant Liberal majority and Speaker of the House to violate Parliament's established rules, close debate, and provide the money. His success in so doing directly laid the foundation for the establishment, within a year's time, of one of Canada's most colorful, enduring, and venerated institutions: the late John George Diefenbaker, leader of the Progressive-Conservative Party and of the anti-American revolt against the policies Howe had epitomized. Diefenbaker's PC administration lasted six years before he was defeated by a combination of his own administrative ineptitude, nativist arrogance, and subtle and unremitting opposition from continentalist backers of the Liberal Party. During his term in office, however, he was successful enough to earn the satisfaction of overhearing President John F. Kennedy, on a visit to Ottawa, refer to him as "that son of a bitch"—at the time, still a most unusual form of diplomatic address.

Howe died on the last day of 1965, and he has been missed; he may have been the last of his kind, as John Angus McDougald —said to be Canada's richest man and certainly one of its most influential—sadly remarked a few years before his own death in 1978:

> C. D. Howe was the last man to bring business and government to-gether. You could deal with C. D. If there was some problem where the government was concerned, you could talk to him. He didn't have to yank in a half a dozen deputies to advise him. He knew what you were talking about. And he'd make a decision just like that. It wouldn't always be in your favour but he knew what it was all about and he could decide so that you could get on with it. I don't know a cabinet minister now who would dare give you a decision without bringing in all his deputies.*

This nostalgia reveals something fairly significant about the attitudes that have helped make foreign economic domination and, specifically, American domination, acceptable to Canadian society. How American C. D. Howe remained at heart I have no idea; he once told a group of distinguished academics who were conferring with him in his office in Parliament, "Oh, you and all the other damn Rhodes scholars! Get the hell out of here!"†— which sounds more American than Canadian in phrasing, though not necessarily in attitude. More to the point, "Winston Churchill is reported to have said 'The British Empire has been sold down the river by C. D. Howe,' when the British prime minister learned that Howe had ordered Eldorado Mining to fill American uranium requirements before Britain's."‡ The combination of Yankee ingenuity, ruthlessness, and inexhaustible drive certainly fits a certain American stereotype. Franklin D. Roosevelt, more admiring than Churchill, commented: "What a quarterback C. D. Howe would have made. If one play fails, he always has another up his sleeve."§ But it was already, for the United States, a stereotype of an earlier era—that of Judge Elbert Gary, per-

---

*Newman, op. cit., p. 46.

†John R. Colombo (ed.), *Colombo's Canadian Quotations* (Edmonton: Hurtig Publishers, 1974), p. 269.

‡Ibid., p. 269.

§Ibid., p. 269.

haps, the steel despot, who died in 1927. Or, more appropriately, Daddy Warbucks: ageless, but even in the 1950s, out of
style. Who was Howe's actual American counterpart under
Roosevelt—Harry Hopkins, a clever man, and sometimes a vain
and sly one? The style was already different in the United States.
Roosevelt, no mean wheelchair quarterback himself, was a fe-
rociously genial despot, who knew better than to try to bully
Congress personally. And by the time Howe's exploits brought
this government down and ended his own political career after
twenty-two years in Parliament, Roosevelt had been dead for
more than twelve years. How did the cabinet minister who finally rose in debate in Parliament to declare, "If there is some
uneasiness in this country about the extent and nature of United
States investment in Canada, this is the wrong place to focus
it,"* get by with it for so long?

It seems clear, as McDougald's remarks illustrate, that the
business community found Howe's approach congenial and his
autocratic methods reassuring rather than threatening. It was
not they, after all, who finally revolted. Howe is remembered
today with pride; one of the most respected economic research
institutes in Canada, widely and frequently cited as an impartial
analyst of trends and problems in the Canadian economy, bears
his name. His patriotism is never questioned, as Henry Kissinger's,
for example, certainly would have been if he had engineered an
arrangement whereby Volkswagen had wound up owning most
of the Chrysler Corporation—and what a boon that would have
been to the American economy! Even ardent and bitter Canadian
nationalists seldom, if ever, accuse Canadian business leaders of
deliberate treachery in selling Canada out; they accuse them,
rather, of having too little sense of what it is to be Canadian and
of being too greedy to care.

Yet, the truth of the matter may, I think, be even harder
to bear for Canadian nationalists concerned with preserving
Canadian identity. I believe that, in behaving as they have,
Canadian business leaders have acted in a manner quintessentially
Canadian—which is not, of course, the same as saying that they
have acted in Canada's best interests, whatever that may mean.

*Ibid., p. 269.

They have certainly had no wish to further American interests. But they have found the ruthlessness, the pragmatism, and the impersonality of American business methods immensely useful to them in furthering their own. American drive effectively complements the more passive Canadian authoritarianism; it gets things done without a whole lot of consultation. In this sense, Canadian elites hire American firms and expertise to do their dirty work for them. The price for this service is very high. Hatchet men always charge a lot, especially when they come back to bury the hatchet.

Conversely, Americans find Canada a happy hunting ground indeed. Do they feel their enterprise constrained at home by American regulations restricting interlocking memberships on boards of directors as conducive to unfair trade practices? Except for banks and trust companies, there are no such restrictions in Canada. Are they hampered and even embarrassed by American regulations requiring disclosure? The Government of Canada discloses nothing about Canadian businesses comparable to the complex and specific information the U.S. Securities and Exchange Commission demands annually from any firm whose securities are traded on an American stock exchange. Even the Royal Commission on Corporate Concentration feels that most of the information required by the SEC should also be made available to the public in Canada, though it did considerately suggest one reservation: "the controversial 10-K requirement of disclosure of remuneration paid to each of the three highest paid corporate officers, and each director who received more than $40,000. Personal information like this should remain confidential."* Since the passage of the Corporations and Labour Unions Returns Act (CALURA) in 1962, Canadian major firms have in fact been required to report to Statistics Canada much of the information required by the U.S. Securities and Exchange Commission; but under CALURA, all but the most general of this information must be kept confidential. This may or may not prevent disclosure—the RCMP has notoriously had very little difficulty in gaining access to information from Canadian income tax returns whose confidentiality is equally and unequiv-

Report of the Royal Commission on Corporate Concentration, p. 325.

ocally protected by law—but it certainly hampers public access and effective self-defense against corporate power.

It nevertheless seems astonishing that the business elites of a country in which economic power is as highly concentrated and society as stratified as in Canada should have abdicated so fully in favor of foreign control. And indeed it would have been incredible if that were, in fact, what had happened. But as Wallace Clement demonstrated in a brilliant analysis in *The Canadian Corporate Elite*,* American economic denomination has never threatened the position of the most powerful Canadian financiers—indeed, it has probably added to it—however much it may have cost the Canadian economy as a whole.

The key to this apparent contradiction lies precisely in the fact that Canadian society is so highly stratified and entry to higher levels so closely guarded. The heights of Canadian economic power were achieved before Canada became highly industrialized, and they have not been successfully scaled. Instead, another parallel economic elite that Clement calls a *comprador* elite has evolved to represent and control American and other foreign interests. It collaborates with the indigenous elite; but it is not permitted to compete effectively with it. It has no comparable independent political power in Canada though, when the two elites work together with such skills as C. D. Howe possessed, they run the country.

Canada's indigenous elite is mercantile, preindustrial, and consolidated its position early on through British portfolio investment. What Canada's first families got rich in, was banking and insurance, railways, utilities, and communications. These, in contrast to manufacturing, have never been open to marauders from abroad, though until recently the indigenous elite defended itself by holding onto its own rather than by relying on government regulation. The rapid and effective response of Walter Gordon and Canadian banking interests to the efforts of what is now Citibank and James Rockefeller to gain a foothold in the Canadian banking industry has already been mentioned; it should be remembered that the Mercantile Bank, which Rockefeller proposed to take over, was already foreign-owned—but by

*Op. cit., pp. 116-22.

Dutch interests the Canadian establishment perceived as innocuous. Behemoths are not easily worsted, and the First National Citibank did ultimately succeed in acquiring control of the Mercantile Bank, but on terms that limited its expansion severely. It is still the only foreign-controlled bank chartered in Canada, and one of the smallest Canadian banks; in 1974 it had twelve branches, less than 1 percent as many as each of the three largest Canadian banks. Relaxation of the controls imposed on the services banks chartered in other countries may legally render in Canada are now under consideration in Parliament. In this connection, it should be recalled that it is far easier for Canadian and provincial legislatures to deal with specific situations, closing particular loopholes or passing enabling legislation, than it would be in the United States, where such specific enactments would usually be ruled unconstitutional. As late as 1964, the legislature of the province of New Brunswick passed an act providing that the West Coast Smelting and Chemical Co., Ltd., controlled, as the legislature itself then was, by the interests of the K. C. Irving family,

> with the approval of the Lieutenant Governor in Council, may, without the consent of the owner thereof or of any person interested therein, enter upon, take possession of, expropriate and use such lands and privileges, easements, servitudes, rights and interests in such and appertaining to such lands, including riparian rights, but excluding mineral rights, as the Company shall deem necessary or useful.*

Legislation repealing this act has since been introduced; but the Irving corporations are still sufficiently a law unto themselves in New Brunswick that they—and they alone—refused to comply with the request of the Royal Commission on Corporate Concentration for "the basic financial information needed for a study that would be made public."†

According to the Royal Commission on Corporate Concentration, in 1974 less than 10 percent of the assets of Canadian corporations in agriculture, forestry and fishing, and transportation were foreign-owned; slightly over 10 percent were foreign-

*Newman, op. cit., p. 233.

†*Report of the Royal Commission on Corporate Concentration*, p. 333.

owned in banking and in printing and publishing—as compared with 44 percent foreign control of the corporations that make the paper for these and other less elegant uses; and 99.8 percent were foreign-controlled in rubber products manufacturing. Tobacco and petroleum and fuel products were also manufactured by corporations over 90 percent foreign-owned; but only 2.4 percent of public utilities and less than one-half of 1 percent of communications facilities were foreign-owned. Thirty-three percent of all nonfinancial industry was foreign-controlled—down from 38 percent in 1967.* The findings of the commission thus strongly support Clement's formulation of, in effect, a bipolar organization of Canadian firms, with foreign investment still excluded from the basic financial and communications industries of Canada. Since Canadian banks so often prefer to lend to large, wealthy American branch plants rather than to riskier new and small Canadian enterprises, foreign-controlled firms are often heavily indebted to Canadian banks, which makes them less independent of Canadian indigenous elites than they appear to be. It also makes indigenous elites richer, and other Canadians poorer, than they would be if Canadian banks were more willing to take chances on budding Canadian enterprise, instead of leaving these risks to be assumed by Canadian government agencies.

If indigenous Canadian elites are resistant to foreign takeover, they are virtually impenetrable to any creatures but male WASPs. The Gray Report observed:

> It was not very long ago that large portions of Canada's population were effectively frozen out of top jobs in Canadian business. Persons who were not of Anglo-Saxon extraction appear to have had more difficulty in penetrating the senior levels of many corporations. They often found it difficult also to obtain the support and assistance for their own smaller businesses from the large corporations, further stultifying their growth capabilities.†

The first six words of the passage quoted suggest that, in this matter at least, the Honorable Herb Gray and his associates

*Ibid., pp. 191-92.

†*Foreign Direct Investment in Canada*, pp. 139-40; quoted in Clement, op. cit., p. 116.

were willing to sacrifice precision to courtesy; the phrase is more suited to a fairy tale. It was not "ago" at all, certainly not when the Gray Report was published in 1972. Clement, in fact, presents data from 1972 showing that the proportion of WASPs in the Canadian elite was almost exactly *twice* their proportion in the total population; the proportion of those of French ethnicity was less than a third of their proportion in the population as a whole. As for other ethnic groups,

> although over one-quarter of Canada's population is made up of ethnic groups other than the two charter groups (26.7 percent), they have almost no representation in the economic elite, except for Jews. From the non-charter groups, there are only 32 Jewish Canadians (4.1 percent) and 10 from other "third" ethnic groups (1.3 percent).*

(The proportion of Jews in the total Canadian population is also about 1.3 percent.) Moreover, the handful of "other" ethnics who are present in Canada's economic elite are nearly all examples of what Clement calls "horizontal mobility": people like Thomas J. Bata, the shoe magnate, who brought their firms to Canada when they came.

Both Clement's more formal and Newman's more personal and anecdotal—but well-documented—account of the recruitment and membership of Canada's economic elite stress its tightly closed structure. The two accounts fully corroborate each other except for minor disagreements. Newman, unlike Clement, sees Canada's exclusive clubs as declining in influence though not in snobbery and is more sympathetic than Clement to the establishment he describes. Born in Vienna, brought to Canada in 1940 at the age of 11, and enrolled in Upper Canada College, Newman must have found in Canada a decidedly more open social structure than he had known as a small child. But both portray an economy, and a polity, dominated by a small and highly concentrated group. Newman, in fact, lists by name and position 173 powerful Canadians who, in his view, constitute "the Canadian Business Establishment"—linked by close personal associations and a largely common world view, self-selected, self-perpetuating, and self-reinforcing by interlocking and overlapping

*Clement, op. cit., pp. 237-38.

corporate ties. *The Report of the Royal Commission on Corporate Concentration* depicts a nearly identical landscape, though with few references to identifiable human figures.

Canadian society is peculiarly consistent. All its institutions are designed or, at least, have evolved to concentrate control at the top, reduce the effectiveness of influences originating at lower levels, and insulate themselves from external stimuli until these have been cleared by persons in authority. This is not, in itself, all that unusual. The statement would be largely true of any highly bureaucratized society, and obviously infinitely more applicable to a totalitarian society like that of the Soviet Union than to Canada. But the situation in Canada is distinguished and complicated by internal paradoxes. One would expect, for example, that so defensive a society would be highly nationalistic; and Canada tries to be and is getting more so. But it is also a society that respects tradition; and its traditions are not its own: the more Canadian it tries to be, the more British— indeed, Victorian—it seems. Less traditional exotic influences, notably American, gain their impact on the Canadian scene by their usefulness to Canadian elites. Sheer size and proximity would make American influence great, anyway; but Canadian society is hard to penetrate without permission. That permission has usually been granted when Canadian elites judged it profitable to do so. They were often correct; their judgments have been shrewd enough; they have been cognizant of the risk involved in bedding down with the proverbial elephant, but have sometimes misstated it. They have not, in any event, been crushed, and protest too much when, as sometimes happens, their offspring develop prominent noses and floppy ears. Sorry about that, but they're still legitimate.

The assimilation of foreign influences tends to be painful and rather strongly resisted in Canada, however. The population is small—about the same as that of California—and its anxiety about being culturally overwhelmed seems realistic. Nevertheless, the comparison may be less revealing than the contrast California otherwise provides. For the people of California, more than those of any place else in the world, have been catholic in their acceptance of a variety of apparently incompatible cultural elements. The result has been not cultural chaos, but a rich, discordant, and diverse pattern of culture, recognized throughout the world as unmistakable in its variety, vulgarity, and vigor. It is not, to be sure, generally admired—though more people probably think they would like to live there than anywhere else they ever heard of. But Californians run no risk that their way of life will be swamped or overrun by exotic elements. On the contrary, it is these elements that make it what it is; and what it is remains unique and, lying as it does beyond the reach of parody, inimitable. Californians have no problem of national identity; the nation has seized California's image and made it its own. Americans, often with loathing, view the state as quintessentially American.

My point is not, of course, to judge the respective merits of Canada and California as places of residence. I feel sure that there are far more satisfied Canadians than satisfied Californians, if only because satisfaction is a characteristic vice among Canadians, as discontent and ambition are among Californians. But I do wish to indicate that a territory hardly more populous than Canada and lacking not only national sovereignty but any yearnings toward independence as a possible bulwark for its identity, has forged such an identity for itself without ever formulating this as a problem and has led the rest of the nation to identify with it not by inspiring emulation or imposing economic domination—New York and Washington are still on top—but by a kind of shock of unconscious recognition which the hinterland is simply unable to withhold. California became, in the age of psychoanalysis, such stuff as dreams are made of—American dreams, surely, but also the dreams of much of the rest of the world, Canada not least. If it has not always been so, it has been so for quite a while. Canada was only twenty-five years old when its daughter, Gladys Marie Smith, was born in Toronto. It is now in better shape than she is; but more people have probably heard of and retain in their minds an image of Mary Pickford.

The point is that California has achieved its cultural preeminence—deplorable as some may find it—precisely because it was so open and eclectic. And the more incongruous its constituent elements became, the more striking and dynamic their pattern. Detractors, accustomed to greater homogeny and better taste, have decried California's culture as synthetic. You'd better believe it.

A synthesis of such compelling power must find its basis in a genuine and deeply rooted cultural pluralism—a necessary though not, of course, sufficient condition. And pluralism is a feature that British culture conspicuously lacks. The lack is understandable. The most hugely successful colonial power in the world, Britain had reason to maintain and defend its insularity— a tendency to "go native," to allow the values and life-styles of an empire on which the sun never set to reflect powerfully back upon the little island on which it rarely shines would have fatally undermined its sense of mission. But, in consequence, the British never learned to incorporate, as more eclectic exploiters have done, the symbols and sometimes even the *virtu* of their victims, and to partake of what their cultures had to offer without patronizing them. London is metropolitan but not cosmopolitan in the sense of New York—or even San Francisco, which is no longer quite a metropolis. In a cosmopolitan center, the various cultural components interact on terms of approximate equality even when they conflict. London is preeminently British; and the British do not suffer other cultures willingly, though they demonstrate their own Britishness by treating them with civility as long as they keep their place.

The British and especially the Scots have transmitted this deficiency in pluralism to their heirs. The result is a peculiar uniformity; foreign influences rapidly disappear and are subtly, or not so subtly, derogated if they persist. This is not, in Canada, an expression of bigotry. That is to be found here, too—where is it not?—but it is not a notably Canadian social trait at any conscious level. The chief justice of Canada is a Jew; the director of the National Gallery in Ottawa is a Chinese-born, American-educated Canadian woman; the director of the Atomic Energy Commission of Canada and former deputy minister of finance— a mandarin indeed—is an ethnic Japanese from Vancouver; the director of the Quebec Symphony is a black paraplegic. Only the native people, and especially the Inuit, seem totally unrepresented in the upper reaches of Canadian society and that, I suspect, is attributable more to the fact that they arouse guilt than to prejudice. Foreigners are not rejected in Canada; but foreignness is; it is something you owe it to yourself to get over. Recently, under the pressure of mounting Canadian nationalism, the Canada Council, which had established a worldwide reputation for autonomy and political independence, introduced a requirement making only Canadian citizens eligible for grants. This was regarded as unfair, and the restriction was modified to restore eligibility to landed immigrants (permanently resident aliens) who had lived in Canada for a shorter time than the period required to make them eligible to apply for Canadian citizenship. Those who, in spite of all temptation to become Canadian, remained what they had been, also remained ineligible.

Canadian culture has therefore received little enrichment from its comparative tolerance. Canadian society, in its treatment of alien influences, is no mosaic, vertical or horizontal. It is more of a melting pot than American society, which has made the phrase a cliché. But in view of the disrespect accorded its exotic components, which are permitted to add very little flavor to the mixture, a better metaphor might be "septic tank." What finally pours into the mainstream of Canadian life is substantially colorless, odorless, noninfectious, and inoffensive, though not entirely sterile. Toronto has its ethnic enclaves: good Anglos go out to Danforth and Pape to watch excellent Greek dancing over coffee and baklava, or down to Kensington Market to see colorful Portuguese life and buy colorful Portuguese or Mediterranean groceries and household objects. Small Asiatic restaurants abound. But it all seems, oddly, both separate and ephemeral, though conspicuous—like a successful vaccination that is really taking, thus insuring that the society will develop resistance to the invaders and preserve itself unchanged. New York, in comparison, does not resist its ethnic groups; it *is* its ethnic groups in continuous interaction. Toronto is of Canada, all compact. New York, notoriously, is "not America"; that's what makes it uniquely American. Of course, so is Disney World. New York embodies the American dream; Disney World the sad reality.

There is doubtless more bigotry to be found in American, and certainly in German, French, Irish, or Soviet, life than in Canadian. English Canadians are not really into bigotry, but they are usually highly ethnocentric. They really do think the English word for anything is its *name*, its ineffable name. What could Shakespeare—a man often too cosmopolitan for his own good—have meant by, "a rose by any other name . . ."? It *hasn't* any other name. Even the Germans and the French, perverse as they are, agree to that. This relatively widespread conviction that what is conventional is not merely appropriate but *right* seems now more firmly established in Canada than in Britain—it is hard to imagine the late Joe Orton as a Canadian playwright, or Tom Stoppard flourishing here unczeched, though both authors are in vogue among Canadian intellectuals. Ethnocentrism, moreover, probably serves to limit rather than encourage bigotry in Canada, as it used to in Britain before the British panicked under the realization that, as an unanticipated aftermath of colonialism, many, many discolored people were bearers of British passports and enjoyed a putative right of entry and residence. Bigotry is bad form. One should not be rude to natives and other foreigners who can't help being what they are.

A respect for social norms sustains certain amenities that please even those who find the norms uncompelling. A society in which there is little public vandalism is also likely to be deficient in more joyful manifestations of spontaneous street life, as Toronto is, compared to New York; but it is undeniably convenient, if a trifle eerie, to find public phone booths equipped with telephone directories nearly every time you want to use one. It is pleasant traveling in economy class on Air Canada even when the plane is full; nobody gouges, and the food and in-flight service are usually good, as if somewhere, even under these conditions, there lurked an idea of what the middle classes are supposed to be entitled to, especially if they don't demand it. If you don't want to fly, the trains are good, too; no longer luxurious but still a little stately, with sit-down dining cars and decent sleeping rooms and lounges and Bingo in the evening with the government providing token prizes. Only Australia has anything better to offer the long distance rail traveler these days.

Social interaction at higher social class levels also seems more satisfactory and, in a sense, more casual in Canada than it is likely to be in the United States. It is still customary to listen to what other people say and respond to it directly though not candidly. Bureaucrats answer letters personally, unless the RCMP or other authority advises them not to. Cooptation is still the name of the game in Canada, and civility is a powerful political weapon. Politeness in dealing with officialdom usually gets you just as far in Canada as it does in the United States—it gets you nowhere, unless you have clout. Rudeness, which *does* sometimes work in the United States, seldom does in Canada because both you and officialdom know that you have no rights with which to back up your threat; you can't take it to court and get anywhere, and it knows you know. Meanwhile, however, your presence will be acknowledged politely—patronizingly if you are a woman or subadult. There is still conversation in Canadian social groups. Wit is valued; dissent is welcomed, debate may be sharp and sarcastic. Again, what makes this acceptable is the assumed consensus on social norms, which insures against subversive insights. Shortly after the Parti Québecois took over the reins of government in Quebec and began to pull to the left, Thomas Galt, chief executive officer of Canada's largest life insurance company, announced in apparent reprisal that Sun Life would pull its head office out of Montreal; his action was severely and in some cases angrily criticized by the federal government and by some Anglophone business leaders who understood that this sort of thing would fuel the flames of separatism. Some, indeed, used exactly this phrase. But the critics also tended to apologize for Galt's action, and his refusal to discuss his decision with the press once it had been announced, as understandable in a foolish old man who had never been heard to speak French in public and had lost touch with social change in Quebec. The tone was one of affectionate reprimand; a Galt, after all, had handled Upper Canada's demands for war reparations from Britain after the War of 1812. Allowances had to be made for his limitations. In fact, Thomas Galt is just a year older than René Lévesque, and nearly two years younger than his Montreal neighbor, Pierre Elliott Trudeau, both of whom understand English quite well. Anglophones seldom make comparable allowance for provincialism when criticizing Premier Lévesque—but, then, they seldom have occasion to.

Everywhere in the world today ordinary people feel powerless, usually for good reason. In Canada, they probably feel this less keenly than in most other places. The government, as indicated, is responsive; if its responses usually change nothing, they still keep one from feeling like a nameless atom. Impotence tends to be somewhat less painful when it is less ego-dystonic. Canadian egos enjoy some protection both because of the prevalent civility and because so little autonomy is expected. Any Detroit black man with thirty cents can walk into a Detroit supermarket, day or night, and buy a bottle of beer to take out and drink. Across the river in Windsor, the richest industrialist cannot; one buys one's beer at government stores, when they're open, and they don't sell single bottles—a sixpack costs about three dollars and they don't stock many brands. To me, the important thing about this example is precisely the fact that it *is* trivial. The more trivial a restriction is, the better evidence it is that the people subject to it have no basic rights. If you can't buy a bottle of beer when you want it in a place where beer, as such, is not only legal but the basic lubricant of working class culture, what can you do? And if you don't mind the government messing with such details of life, where do you stop it? But Canadian acceptance of petty regulation again reflects the absence of pluralism from the central pattern of Canadian values. People here are likely to argue that an onerous rule should be changed; but not that there shouldn't be one, and certainly not that it is silly and dangerous to impose on everyone rules that merely reflect the folkways of the dominant culture. Jews in Canada have enjoyed and shall continue to enjoy religious freedom; but the Supreme Court has ruled that the Lord's Day is *Sunday*. You may observe Saturday too, if you want to.

There is really no need, then, to argue about these things, much less for endless litigation. Attorneys for the federal government are now arguing (in August 1979) against the land claims of the Inuit on the grounds that the Inuit had no conception of property rights and private property and therefore have no basis for a claim that can be pressed in Canadian courts. The land was never theirs. The logic is breathtaking in both its audacity and its ethnocentricity. It seems equally clear that the attorneys for the Crown, having no conception of *chutzpah*, cannot be charged with it.

In a rather similar display of self-confidence,

the president of the Atomic Energy Control Board told an Ontario

Government committee investigating the safety of nuclear power plants not to burden the board with too many requests for information.

Jon Jennekens told the select committee on Hydro affairs yesterday that the control board, the body that issues licenses for nuclear power plants, is understaffed and that its regulatory responsibilities are more important than the committee hearings. . . . He said the board will issue written reports to the committee but that those reports will not contain any new information. "Written presentations will be based largely upon existing documentation."

He said the board "will endeavor to comply with reasonable requests for additional documentation." He asked, however, "that such requests be minimized since each additional hour expended on preparing written documents will detract from our licensing and compliance activities."

The committee listened quietly and without comment as Mr. Jennekens read from a prepared statement.*

English Canadians have been doing so, with occasional exceptions, for a long time now. Most of them would, I believe, maintain that their quiescent style has enhanced their freedom, not restricted it. Canadians don't spend as much time and effort fighting one another as Americans do, so they don't get in each other's way as much; they don't waste as much energy on anger and litigation, so they can get more done in a quiet way than Americans can by unrestrained hyperactivity. The parliamentary system permits the government of the day to put its programs into action: Parliament does not burst into derisive laughter every time the prime minister opens his mouth, as the Congress does in response to presidential proposals. The ubiquitous Government of Canada does not merely restrict; it also establishes order, which is the fundamental precondition of freedom. You are not free to walk about the city if you have reason to fear being mugged or shot. You are not free to do anything much in your later years if you are continually dogged by threat of catastrophic illness. In these important respects Canadians enjoy far more freedom than Americans.

Most important of all, the pace of life in Canada encourages reflection and informed choice; there is more privacy, still, even

*Mary Kate Rowan, "Too Busy to Give Data, AECB Head Tells MPPs," *Toronto Globe and Mail*, July 7, 1979.

though Canadian law and Canadian courts have established no *right* to privacy, as American law has. Life in Canada is more relaxed; the unconscious need not waste so much of itself in defensive operations and can serve more effectively as a guardian at crucial moments and during the quiet times between them. Wisdom is possible, though optional.

All this is quite true, and one could hardly exaggerate its importance. There is, finally, the stubborn reality of the senses. Despite the enormous potential for oppression the Canadian system affords, I have not been and do not feel oppressed here; and the years I have spent in this country have been the happiest I have known. But, then, having been schooled the hard way in the costs and the sometimes devious ways of liberty, Americans can *afford* to enjoy Canada. The rate of exchange is favorable to us. Canadians may find this indulgence too expensive.

But that, clearly, is for Canadians to decide. It is also—depite the continuous *kvetching* about their helplessness in the toils of the American giant, which leaves the bemused observer wondering how Canada would fare against Nicaragua in the Pan-American Games—something Canadians are quite capable of deciding themselves. Liberty may be sought and defended in many different ways, formal and informal. Different cultures, moreover, assign liberty different ranks in their scale of values. Canadians assign it a high rank, formally; but they do not, in the event, grant it precedence. And even that quintessential American, the late Vince Lombardi, significantly failed to say, "Liberty isn't everything; it's the only thing": he said *"winning."* The worst thing about Americans is that we can't be trusted to see the difference. But there is a connection between freedom and victory—even between freedom and combat readiness—which might well receive more emphasis than Canadians have traditionally recognized.

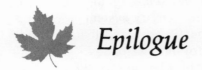 *Epilogue*

In the middle of December 1979, the Progressive-Conservative government of Canada was defeated in Parliament on an issue sufficiently fundamental to be regarded, unmistakably, as a formal test of confidence. It fell. As of now—New Year's Day, 1980—this has not made any of the statements in this book inaccurate (though some doubtless were already). The new general election has been scheduled for February 18, 1980; until then, the incumbent government remains in office in a kind of caretaker status. Charles Joseph Clark is still prime minister of Canada and is making every effort to remain so. By the time this book is published, he may have succeeded.

If he fails, Pierre Elliott Trudeau will become prime minister again. The New Democratic Party, unblemished by the scars of federal office, is now the only national political party in Canada that makes any sense; but making sense does not get you elected. The party is expected to make significant gains in February, perhaps even becoming the official opposition; but it does seem inconceivable that it could win enough seats to form the government in the next election. As between the Liberal and Progressive-Conservative parties, it seems to me impossible to judge at this time which has the better chances. Recent public opinion polls show the Liberals with a large lead in the popular vote. But regional party preferences are so firmly fixed in Canada that large shifts in the popular vote make very little difference in the final outcome. There is no way the PC can make substantial gains in Quebec; as of now, the party is planning to campaign hard in only seven of Quebec's seventy-five ridings. And west of

Ontario, Trudeau is regarded as an Ayatollah, though that is not as severe a handicap under a parliamentary system as under a presidential system, since westerners who vote Liberal are not asked to—indeed, cannot—vote for him personally.

For a brief time it seemed that the question would not arise. Late this past fall, Mr. Trudeau renounced the leadership of the Liberal Party for personal reasons, which doubtless included the wish to spare the party the burden of his increasingly ambiguous charisma. It is widely, and almost certainly accurately, surmised that it was the Liberal Party's temporarily leaderless condition that tempted the Progressive-Conservative government to its fate by leading it to suppose that the Liberals would not dare to oppose it strongly enough to bring about a general election at a time when they were in severe disarray. But they did. Faced with a budget that was extremely unpopular and that sounded more absurd than it was, the Liberals and the New Democratic Party pulled themselves together and pulled together. Herb Gray, the Liberal finance minister, moved an amendment to the motion to accept the budget, which was critical of it. Robert Rae, NDP finance critic, moved an amendment to this amendment, which changed the criticism to outright condemnation. Together, the two parties had enough votes to defeat the minority PC government unless the five Francophone Social-Credit members from rural ridings of Quebec voted with it.

The SoCreds had done so in the past; being on the far right of Canada's political spectrum, they had nowhere else to go. But they had been treated with scant respect in the House of Commons. Numbering too few to be recognized as an official political party under Canada's rules of parliamentary procedure, their rights of debate had been sharply limited; the Speaker of the House, James Jerome, Liberal member for Sudbury, Ontario, had even refused to recognize SoCred members during Question Period. Since they had no place else to go, they didn't go anywhere. They stayed in their offices when the division bell rang, summoning the members to vote; and they all abstained. The government's new excise tax, rubbing salt in the wounds inflicted by rising oil prices in the interests of discouraging consumption would, they said, be murderous to their rural constituents, who had to depend on their cars. It also seemed a poor way to discourage Quebec separatism, and the SoCred members are federalists.

The SoCreds abstained. The Liberals and the NDP voted. One PC member, reputedly miffed at having been passed over for a cabinet post, failed to show. Flora MacDonald, the minister for external affairs, was caught up in an external affair in Europe and could not get back in time. The government fell.

Faced with the immediate necessity of finding a leader, the Liberals hurriedly canvassed possibilities. Leadership conventions take time to organize and are inherently divisive; the two top contenders—with Trudeau *hors concours*—were both top Toronto corporation lawyers. One of them is notably more Liberal than the other; but neither is well-suited to bear the standard of the ordinary, inflation-ravaged Canadian. The Party Executive urged Mr. Trudeau to reconsider and firmly promised support if he would do so; and Trudeau spent the weekend privately wrestling with his conscience.

Deprived of the challenges of leadership, the latter had quickly grown flaccid. Trudeau won easily. No longer leaderless, its loins well-girded, the Liberal Party of Canada is again arrayed in all its glory—though it has lost some of its more effective candidates, who have no wish to run for public office again after only seven months. Those who were defeated have returned to their private careers and cannot afford to interrupt them again. Speaker Jerome, who had compromised himself by his agreement to retain the Speaker's chair under the Clark government at a time when his party badly needed his vote in Opposition, has declared that he will accept an unspecified federal appointive post, which Prime Minister Clark still has the power to confer, rather than run again.

So, matters fall into place; but not quite in the same pattern. Trudeau is campaigning much more quietly, attempting where possible to thrust local Liberal candidates into the spotlight. The most enigmatic, and politically crucial, area of the country is clearly Ontario. Although the provincial government there has been conservative since 1943, Ontario, with ninety-five seats in Parliament at its disposal—more than any other province—is the only province in Canada that regularly, though inconsistently, returns a substantial number of members under the banner of each of the three major parties. It is, in short, always the "swing" province, with the most hotly contested federal campaigns.

In 1980, Ontario's role should be especially crucial because the position of its premier, William G. Davis—probably the most powerful PC politician in Canada—has changed with respect to his federal counterpart, Joe Clark. Clark won with the aid of Davis's consistent and insistent support, which Davis, bound by the constraints of party loyalty, has again promised. But the two men have become political adversaries, for reasons of demography, which are more stubborn, politically, than any personality factors that might be involved. Ontario, of course, is Canada's most industrialized province, and its currently troubled economy is heavily dependent on a massive supply of relatively cheap Alberta oil as well as on protective tariffs for its fairly diversified industry—tariffs that put economies like Alberta's, more dependent on extraction than on manufacturing, at a disadvantage. The economic interests of the two provinces are irreconcilably in conflict. Clark is himself an Albertan, his cultural and political ties tend to be to that province, and his policies, insofar as their thrust can be discerned, seem so far to have favored Alberta. Under the new budget, oil prices would have risen more rapidly than the present, still binding, agreement provides, while the Clark government's determination to turn over the government oil company, Petrocan, substantially to private investors, would deprive the federal government of its most important leverage on petroleum pricing and development policy. Davis is expected to support the Tory campaign effort more deliberately than he did in 1979. No man now recognizes more clearly than he the importance, morally as well as economically, of conserving energy.

The New Democratic Party is, and has been, relatively strong in Ontario; this election it should win a lot more seats. But at the expense of which major party? Ontario's nearly forty years of PC provincial government are in large measure a reflection of NDP strength, just as Conservative chances in Britain were temporarily enhanced as the growth of the Labour Party sapped the British Liberals before Labour grew strong enough to win for itself. But this time, lack of zeal on the part of the

Davis machine might well allow seats the PC won narrowly in the 1979 federal election to pass into NDP hands, with the consequence of again returning the Liberals to office. Davis, I should judge, has nothing to fear from antagonizing the federal Progressive-Conservative Party. Except for Alberta, he is bigger than it is—though Canada may not be big enough for both him and Peter Lougheed, Alberta's PC premier. The roots of conflict between Alberta and Ontario go much deeper, economically, than those between Ontario and Quebec; and there is no language barrier to insulate them.

All this is interesting, especially if you live in Canada; but I don't think it adds any new, significant factors to our understanding of what Canada is and how it works. Looking back on the seventies, it does seem that the most cheerful and soothing sound—almost the only soothing and cheerful sound—to be heard during the decade was the recurrent patter of governments falling—whether on hot tin roofs or just on evil times. Canada, too, had something to contribute to this euphony, and one would not like to have seen it fail to take its due place in the procession of nations.

So it goes.

 *Index*